A VISUAL HISTORY OF THE WORLD

A VISUAL HISTORY OF THE WORLD'S ENDURING MYSTERIES

ROSEN PUBLISHING

JOAN SORIANO CAMPOS

This edition published in 2017 by
The Rosen Publishing Group, Inc.
29 East 21st Street
New York, NY 10010

Library of Congress Cataloging-in-Publication Data

Names: Soriano Campos, Joan.
Title: A visual history of the world's enduring mysteries / Joan Soriano Campos.
Description: New York : Rosen Publishing, 2017. | Series: A visual history of the world | Includes bibliographical references and index.
Identifiers: ISBN 9781499465785 (library bound)
Subjects: LCSH: Antiquities—Miscellanea—Juvenile literature.| Archaeology—Miscellanea—Juvenile literature. | Civilization—Miscellanea—Juvenile literature.
Classification: LCC CC171.C36 2017 | DDC 930.1—dc23

Manufactured in Malaysia

Metric Conversion Chart

1 inch = 2.54 centimeters; 25.4 millimeters
1 foot = 30.48 centimeters
1 yard = .914 meters
1 square foot = .093 square meters
1 square mile = 2.59 square kilometers
1 ton = .907 metric tons
1 pound = 454 grams
1 mile = 1.609 kilometers

1 cup = 250 milliliters
1 ounce = 28 grams
1 fluid ounce = 30 milliliters
1 teaspoon = 5 milliliters
1 tablespoon = 15 milliliters
1 quart = .946 liters
355 degrees F = 180 degrees Celsius

Original Idea Nuria Cicero
Editorial Coordination Alberto Hernández
Editorial Team Alberto Moreno de la Fuente, Luciana Rosende, Virginia Iris Fernández, Pablo Pineau, Matías Loewy, Joan Soriano, Mar Valls, Leandro Jema
Proofreaders Marta Kordon, Edgardo D'Elio
Design María Eugenia Hiriart
Layout Laura Ocampo, Clara Miralles, Paola Fornasaro

Photography Age Fotostock, Getty Images, Science Photo Library, National Geographic, Latinstock, Album, ACI, Cordon Press
Illustrations and Infographics Trexel Animation, Trebol Animation,
WOW Studio, Sebastián Giacobino, Néstor Taylor, Nuts Studio, Steady in Lab, 3DN, Federico Combi, Pablo Aschei, Leonardo César, 4D News, Rise Studio, Ariel Roldán, Dorian Vandegrift, Zoom Desarrollo Digitales, Marcelo Regalado.

Contents

Introduction

Few topics hold arouse so much fascination in the human being as the unanswered questions about the past: **lost civilizations**, undeciphered scripts, myths that could have real backgrounds, missing tombs, murders with unknown perpetrators, treasures hidden from human greed and surrounded by legend.

Puzzles are always the result of a lack of evidence. The absence or scarcity of written documents, material remains or other kind of evidence welcomes different **interpretations**, sometimes full of fantasy and devoid of accuracy. Some mysteries have caused much controversy in the scientific field itself, and for years, or even centuries, they have fueled passionate discussions and **hypotheses**.

The science with greater capacity to resolve these questions of our past is archaeology, thanks to which we can distinguish real from fabled events, resorting to the analysis and reconstruction of remains, to excavation and to the restoration of papyri and parchments, among others. A branch of this science that allows significant verification is called Experimental **Archaeology**. It employs techniques in the same conditions in which they would have been employed at that certain historical time. This is the case of the archaeologists who implemented hypothetical systems for the transfer of the large stone blocks of Stonehenge (United Kingdom) or the gigantic sculptures of Easter Island, and the method of tracing the geoglyphs of Nazca (Peru).

In turn, technological advances have allowed archaeology to resume some **research** that had reached a dead-end due to lack of essential information with new and sophisticated techniques. Dating has served to dispel many **doubts**. In addition, the tomography and the DNA analysis have been instrumental in clarifying famous enigmas such as the cause of death of Pharaoh Tutankhamun and the identification of the bodies of members of the Russian royal family, the Romanov.

In some cases, the new insights pose unprecedented **questions** while closing other. And it is likely that some mysteries will never be solved, for the enjoyment of those who love the puzzle mysteries of our history.

Chronology

1947

▶ DEAD SEA SCROLLS
Announcement of the discovery of manuscript scrolls that reveal secrets about the life of Jews and Christians in the time of Jesus.

1971

▶ CAMELOT
Excavations by archaeologist Leslie Alcock reveal that the hill in Cadbury Castle could host the famous Camelot Court of King Arthurt.

1969

▶ NAZCA
Archaeologist Maria Reiche published a thorough description and interpretation of the mysterious Nazca lines.

1969

▶ EL DORADO
The finding of the Muisca Raft within a vessel corroborates the theory that El Dorado existed near the Guatavita Lake (Colombia).

1978

▶ GOSPEL OF JUDAS
The Codex Tchacos was found in El Minya (Egypt) . One of the texts of this ancient papyrus calls into question a basic belief of Christianity: the betrayal of Jesus by Judas.

1990

▶ DINOSAURS
Identification of the Chicxulub crater (Mexico), created by the meteorite that supposedly caused the extinction of the dinosaurs about 65 million years ago.

1991

▶ THE ROMANOVS

The grave with the remains of Tsar Nicholas II and his family, executed in 1918, was located in Yekaterinburg (Russia).

1995

▶ TROY

After his excavations at Troy, archaeologist Manfred Korfman gave credence to the theory of the great siege narrated by Homer.

1998

▶ THE GREAT FLOOD

Geologists William Ryan and Walter Pitman found evidence of a great flood that could match the biblical Flood in the area closest to the Euphrates and the Tigris.

2002

▶ STONEHENGE

Discovery of the Tomb of the Amesbury Archer, a mysterious nobleman from continental Europe who may have participated in the construction of Stonehenge.

2007

▶ CIA DOCUMENTS

The Central Intelligence Agency declassified the so-called "Family Jewels," secret documents on its activities between 1953 and 1973.

2009

▶ ADOLF HITLER

The Kremlin admits to the destruction in 1970 of the remains of the Nazi dictator, which had been secretly buried in Magdeburg in 1946.

2010

▶ TUTANKHAMUN

The published DNA studies reveal the likely cause of death of the Pharaoh: malaria, aggravated by a bone disease.

Chapter 1

Enigmas of Antiquity

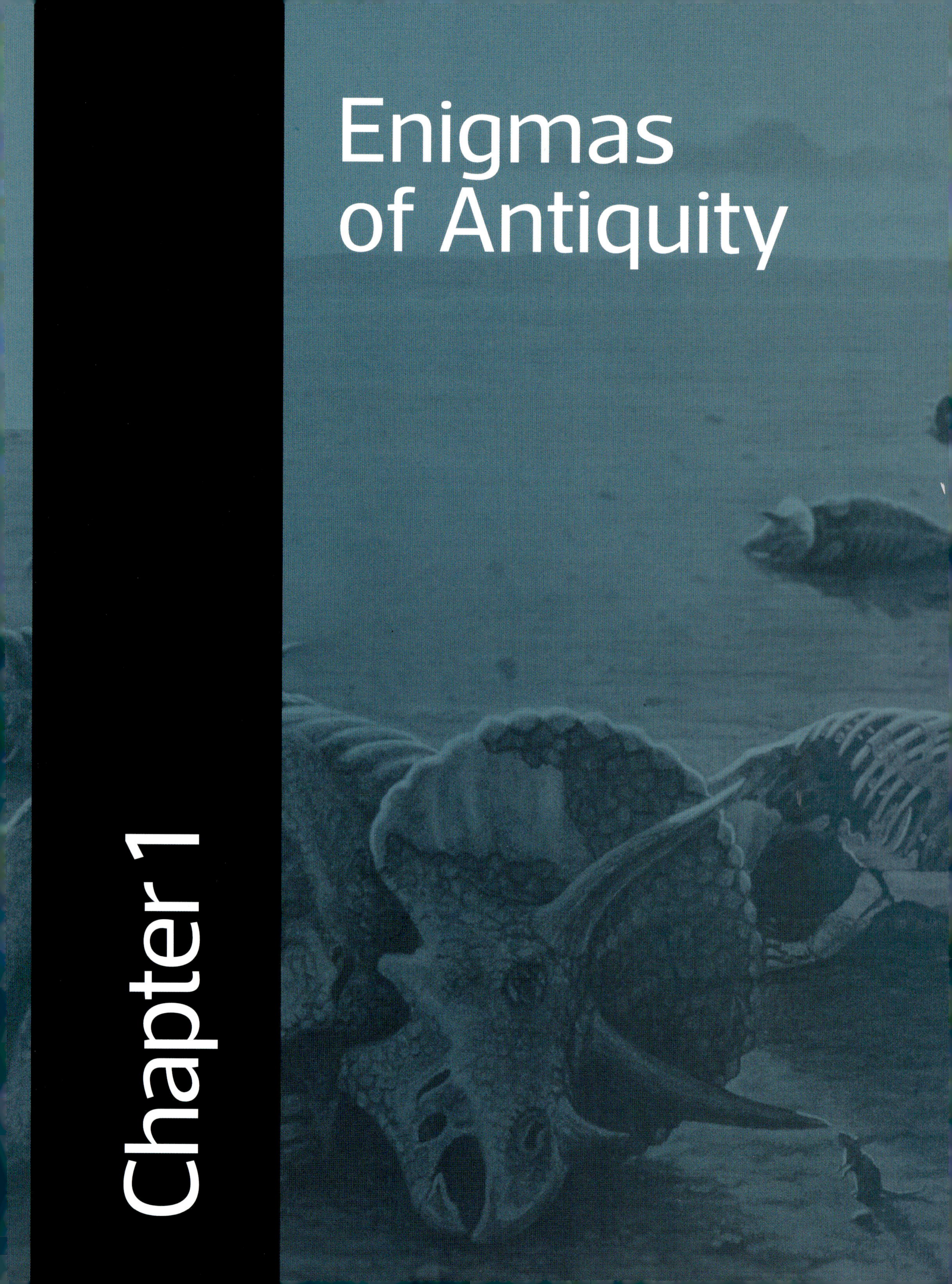

Nothing is more implacable than the passage of time when erasing the traces of our ancestors or modifying space, the specific environment inhabited by previous civilizations. It is therefore in the ancient world history where researchers encounter greater uncertainties, sometimes with enigmas of such magnitude that no even plausible hypotheses can be established.

The very origin of man is already in itself one of the major mysteries surrounding Humanity, although not the first, as many other unknowns precede it, from the very formation of the Universe to the extinction of dinosaurs.

Posing the right questions in an accurate fashion, with meticulous analyzes and toiling interpretations that require exercising a creative imagination more than ever, researchers of the most distant past try to solve questions like the enigmatic disappearance of the Neanderthals, the construction of the pyramids of Egypt or the countless secrets connected with Christianity, the myths of which sometimes rest on real events that archaeologists and historians try to differentiate from existing fables in sacred books, with origins in oral tradition.

The Origin of Man

Who are our ancestors? How long have we been human? There is no doubt of the animal origin of our species, but also science and religion have agreed on another point: we descend from Adam and Eve.

Common Ancestors

Recent research in biology and genetics has shown that we all come from the same Adam and the same Eve (though they are much older than those in the Bible), a conclusion resulting from the analysis of a shared genetic chain. According to this theory of the origin of the species, the first modern humans, *Homo sapiens*, appeared in Africa between 100,000 and 200,000 years ago.

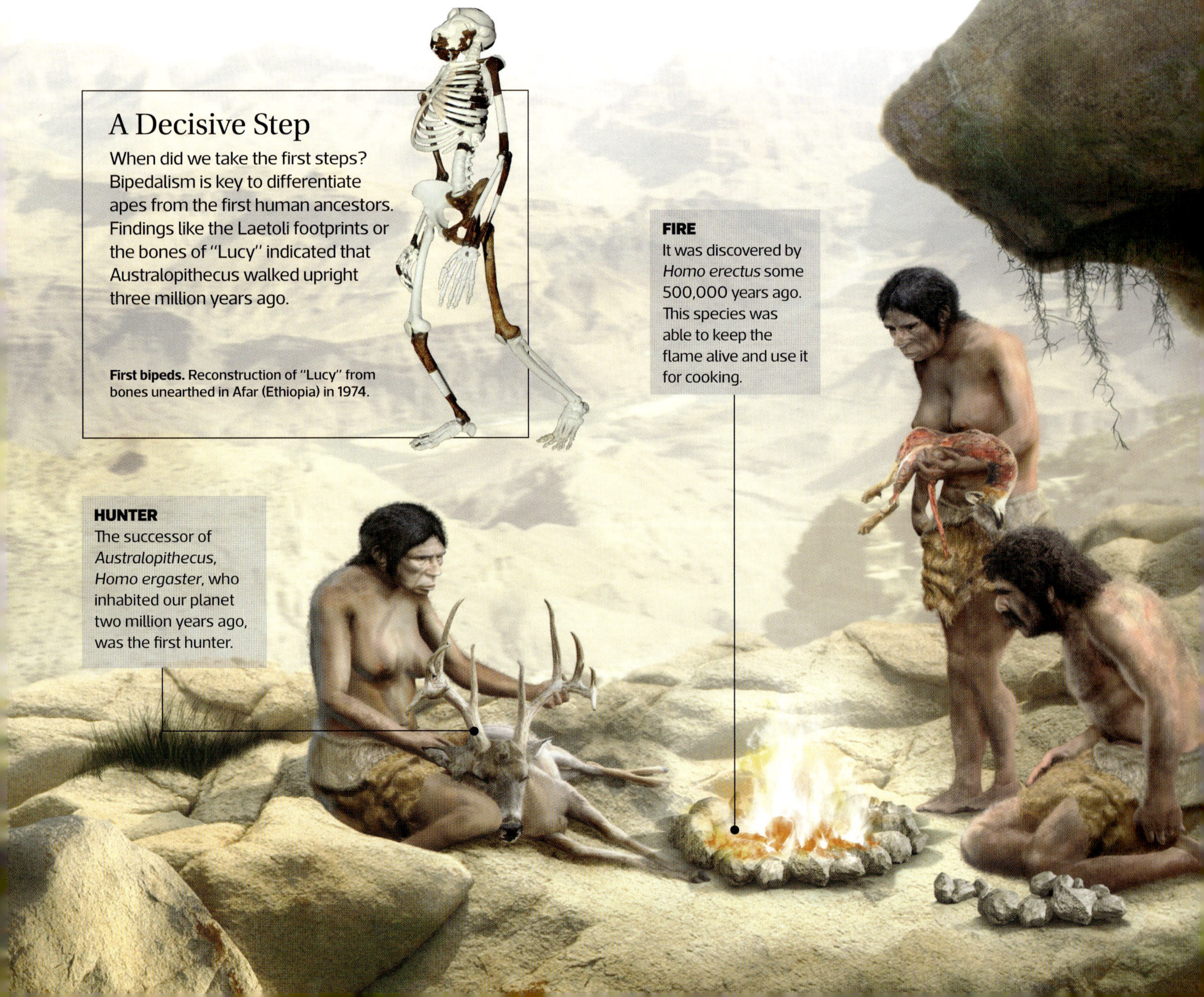

A Decisive Step

When did we take the first steps? Bipedalism is key to differentiate apes from the first human ancestors. Findings like the Laetoli footprints or the bones of "Lucy" indicated that Australopithecus walked upright three million years ago.

First bipeds. Reconstruction of "Lucy" from bones unearthed in Afar (Ethiopia) in 1974.

FIRE
It was discovered by *Homo erectus* some 500,000 years ago. This species was able to keep the flame alive and use it for cooking.

HUNTER
The successor of *Australopithecus*, *Homo ergaster*, who inhabited our planet two million years ago, was the first hunter.

TOOLS
Between 2.5 and 1.5 million years ago, *Homo habilis* began using carved pieces of rock to chop the meat and cut hard surfaces.

When Did We Start Talking?

Oral communication emerged 2.5 million years ago, but not the language. It is believed that, a hundred thousand years ago, humans were speaking a shared proto-language, which diversified and became more sophisticated, allowing the *Homo* genus to get more sociable, sensitive and intelligent.

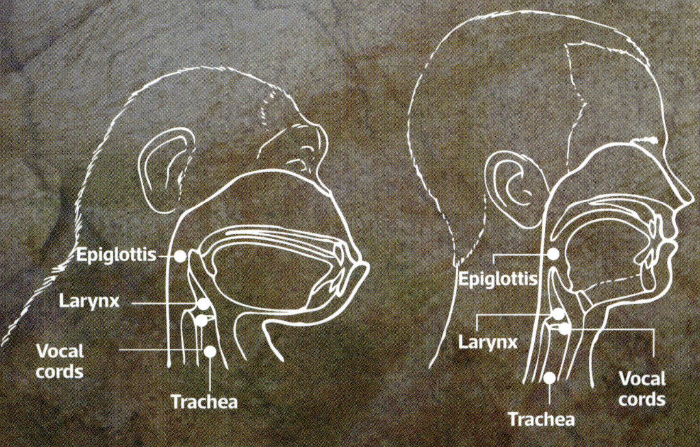

Vocal apparatus. In humans, the larynx is lower in comparison with apes. This facilitated the vocal cords the production of a greater variety of sounds.

From Hominid to Human

Science has established that we have been "humans" for about 2.5 million years when, at some point in the Palaeolithic Era, within a chain of hominids that lasted seven million years, a scavenger species appeared with a much larger brain than that of their predecessors, being capable of making stone tools. This is the *Homo* genus.

Constant evolution. Several models of skulls of different species.

The End of the Dinosaurs

The mysterious phenomenon that ended the age of dinosaurs must have left a grim scenario. It made no distinction between large or small beings, and no continent on the planet was safe. Only birds avoided that great catastrophe.

Cataclysm

Whether a terrestrial or extraterrestrial event, a series of volcanic eruptions or a meteor shower (or a combination of both elements), it is certain that the catastrophe that ended the Mesozoic Era was one of the largest extinctions in the history of planet Earth. About 75% of animal species disappeared.

TOXIC GASES
It is believed that the impact of a meteorite produced a thick blanket of dust that clouded the sky permanently, hindering photosynthesis and disrupting the food chain. Furthermore, the atmosphere would have been laden with toxic gases.

FATAL VICTIMS
The Large North American Triceratops were among the victims of the natural phenomenon. United States palaeontologists have documented fields with hundreds of fossils of this species.

GREAT CEMETERY
Over the millennia, the land surface became a gigantic cemetery that, in prime locations on the planet, preserved the remains of these dinosaurs as fossils.

In Search of Cloning

In theory, science could revive a dinosaur if it had soft tissue or stable DNA samples. At the end of the last century, the discovery of a tick of 90 million years of age in a piece of amber and the analysis of a dinosaur egg by Chinese scientists made hope flare up, but there were no final conclusions.

Looking for DNA. Molecular biologist Chen Zhangliang analysing a dinosaur egg.

BLAST WAVE
Artistic representation of the Chicxulub crater, the result of a meteorite impact.

The Impact Site

In 1990, some geologists identified the Chicxulub crater, with a diameter of 180 km, in the Yucatan Peninsula (Mexico), as the place where the meteorite causing the extinction of dinosaurs would have impacted 65.5 million years ago. But there are more theories. In 1997, another crater was discovered on the floor of the Indian Ocean, 50 times larger than the Mexican crater, and from the same era, where another devastating meteorite hit.

Therizinosaurus. Therapod of the Maniraptora group, considered a distant relative of birds.

Do Birds Descend from Dinosaurs?

In a brilliant article published in 1973 in *Nature* magazine ("The Ancestry of Birds"), U.S. palaeontologist John Ostrom listed 20 morphological features present in birds and dinosaurs, which would provide the basis to support that birds are direct descendants of carnivorous dinosaurs similar to the Velociraptor.

Neanderthal Extinction

Neanderthals lived in Europe and western Asia during 200,000 years ago, in the Middle Palaeolithic. For about 5,000 years, they shared their territory with *Homo sapiens*. Then they disappeared from the face of the Earth without even science knowing why.

Natural Selection

Neanderthals became extinct about 20,000 years ago. Some scientists argue that the emergence of *Homo sapiens* in Europe, with whom they shared the continent for 5,000 years, would have been the cause of the end of the Neanderthals, either for being assimilated (the *Homo sapiens* were ten times more numerous) or for being unable to compete for resources and food. Another possibility is that they could have been killed in violent clashes with Sapiens or contracted new diseases against which they lacked defences.

Difficult coexistence. Recreation of a group of Neanderthals and *Homo sapiens* around 35,000 years ago.

Morphological Differences

The main differences between Neanderthal and modern humans are found in the skull. Dolichocephalic and larger, it has more pronounced features, such as the distinctive and primitive superciliary arch, a lower forehead and the powerful jaw with almost no chin. In addition, the nasal septum is higher and the nostrils, larger.

Robustness. With an average height of 1.65 m for males and 1.55 m for women, Neanderthal men had a more robust appearance than *Homo sapiens*.

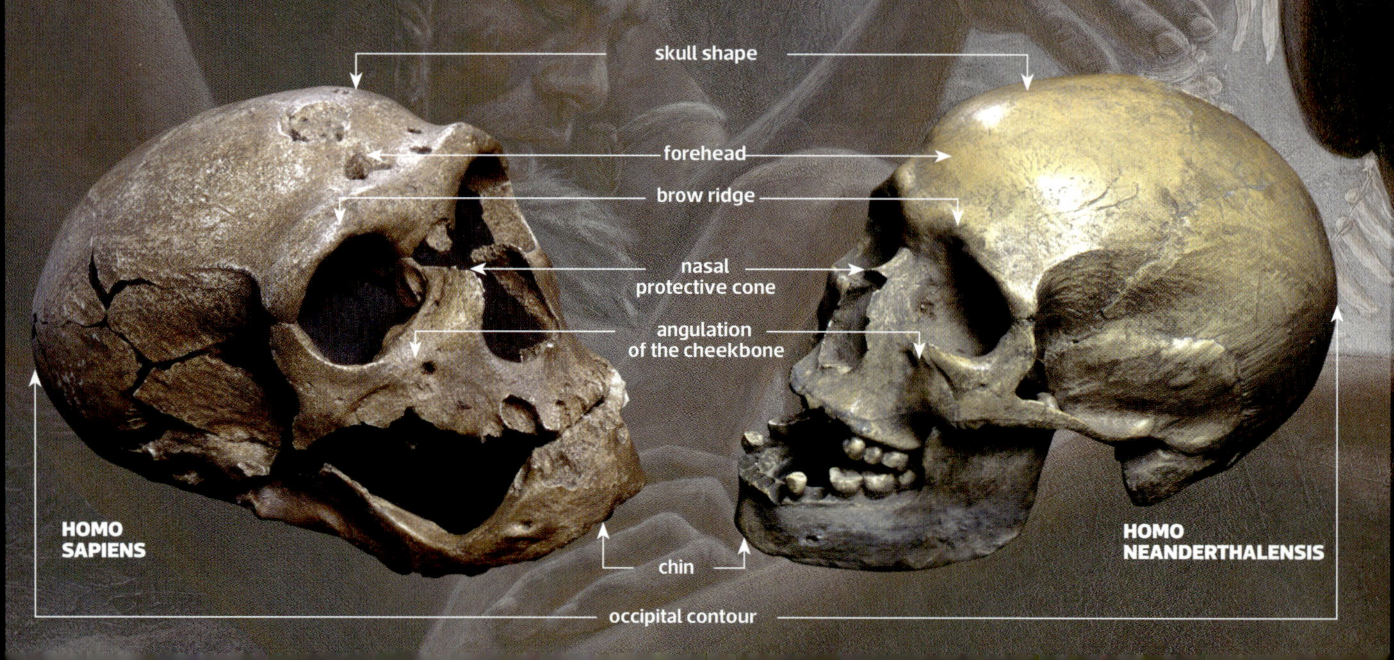

Secluded

The archaeological Mousterian remains (dating back to between 34,000 and 31,000 years ago) in the subarctic Russian town of Byzovaya, when Europe was occupied almost entirely by *Homo sapiens*, seems to prove that Neanderthals were cornered by their contemporaries.

RESISTANCE TO COLD
Some scientists have ruled out the theory that Neanderthals succumbed by the harshness of the last major glaciation. They believe that they were adapted to cold temperatures.

FEATURES
Neanderthals were blond or redheads, had a broad chest, thick bones, short limbs, a low, sloping forehead, a chinless jaw and a large skull.

WERE THERE MIXES?
While some geneticists maintain that there was no miscegenation between Neanderthals and sapiens, others say that up to 4% of the DNA of modern humans is of Neanderthal origin.

Stonehenge Keys

During the Neolithic, Atlantic Europe and especially the British Isles were filled with simple circular or elliptical monolithic constructions called *cromlechs*, the function, origin and construction of which still contain many mysteries.

Its Builders

The construction of Stonehenge lasted over a thousand years. It is estimated that the third construction phase demanded the equivalent of 300 men working ten hours a day. It is believed that most of the workers (also dedicated to agriculture and livestock) lived in the neighboring village of Durrington Walls. Although other peoples like the Egyptians or the Sumerians were more advanced, the lintel structures with carved stones of Stonehenge demonstrate the ability of this British generation of the Neolithic.

Origin of Stones

The analysis of the stones of Stonehenge revealed that siliceous sandstone monoliths (up 40 tonnes) came from a site located about 30 km, and 80 bluestone blocks were from the Preseli mountains (Wales) to 240 km away. In addition, they lacked animal traction for transportation, and the path is difficult.

Blue stones. They are thus named because they acquire a bluish hue when wet by rain.

PERFECT FIT
Lintels were assembled to the monoliths by fitting concave with convex shapes. The implementation of this tongue and groove technique so far ahead of the Neolithic period is surprising.

CELEBRATION
It is believed that Stonehenge was a ceremonial center created by the Celtic Druids. Consequently, Celtic religious groups and hippies celebrate with rituals the arrival of the summer solstice every year.

The Strange "Amesbury Archer"

In 2002, a group of archaeologists discovered two prehistoric graves in the town of Amesbury, a little more than 3 kilometers away from Stonehenge. The remains, which date back to around 2300 BC, belonged to a man in his 40s and a younger relative. What was surprising was that the analysis of the teeth revealed that the "archer" was not a native of England, but of the Swiss Alps.

A rich trousseau. Along with the bones, gold jewellery, pottery, copper knives and arrows were found.

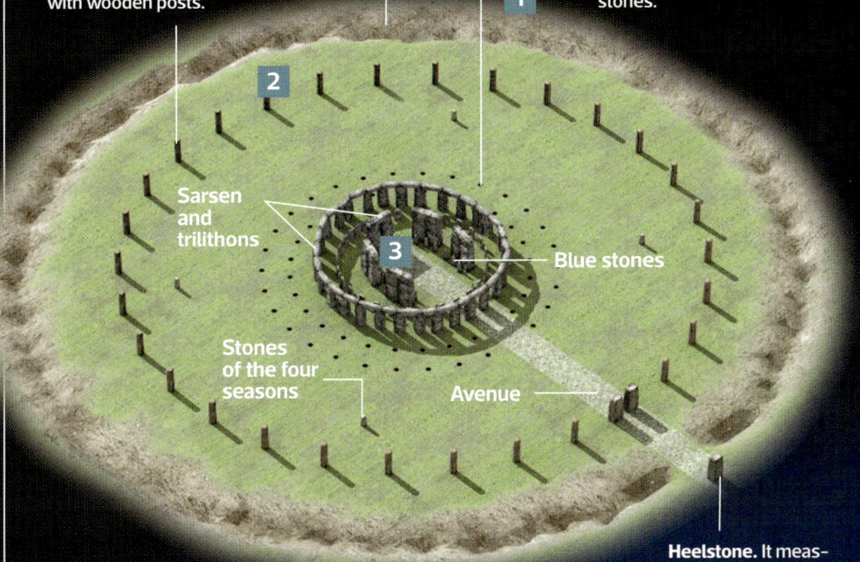

The Construction Phases

Historian and archaeologist Richard Atkinson directed the excavations at Stonehenge from 1940 to 1964. He concluded that the monument was built on three essential phases.

1 **2950 BC -2900 BC.** By the Mid-Neolithic, the embankment was prepared and the circular ditch was dug. Afterwards, the so-called "Aubrey Circle" was designed within the embankment.

2 **2900 BC -2550 BC** For 500 years, the Aubrey Circle held wooden posts. Later, some of the holes were filled with cremated remains.

3 **2550 BC -1600 BC** In the third phase, the stone circles were completed. There were constant changes up to the final position of the menhirs and trilithons.

What Was its Function?

There is no categorical certainty about the function of Stonehenge, but its alignment with the summer solstice sunrise suggests that it was an observatory or a temple dedicated to the Sun. Another hypothesis, supported by the discovery of human remains buried around the monument, indicates that it may have been a large funeral center for elites.

The Pyramids of Egypt

How could a stone construction as the Pyramid of Khafre, which until the 19th century was the highest in the world, be erected thousands of years ago? What techniques were implemented by the Egyptians? Scholars are still looking for definitive answers.

Construction Process

Most Egyptologists agree that the construction of the pyramids had to follow a four-step process: land levelling, alignment (they applied their knowledge of astronomy to map and orient the lines of the pyramid), building the underground chamber and building the pyramid with large blocks of stone. Almost certainly, ramps were used to work at height.

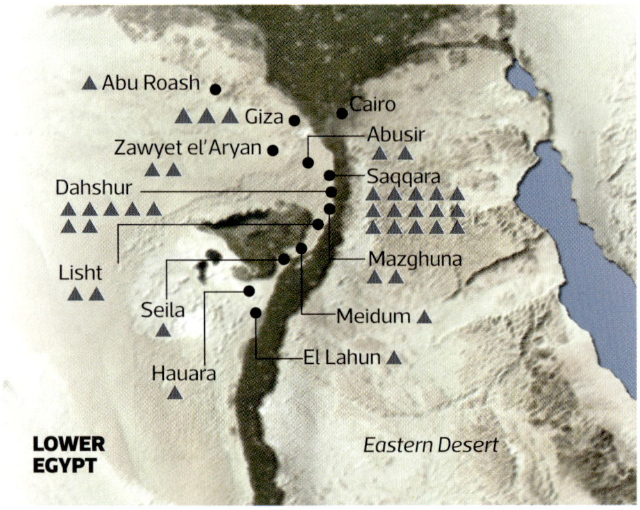

Main Egyptian Pyramids

As the map shows, all the pyramids are found on the west bank of the Nile River, the place of the dead, and near a town, possibly for the need to count with an infrastructure for their complex construction.

Planning and Speed

The pyramids must have needed an advanced planning technique and a steady supply of resources to ensure their completion during the life of the kings. Tons of rocks, some from the place and others brought from several miles away, needed to be moved and stacked to build the monuments.

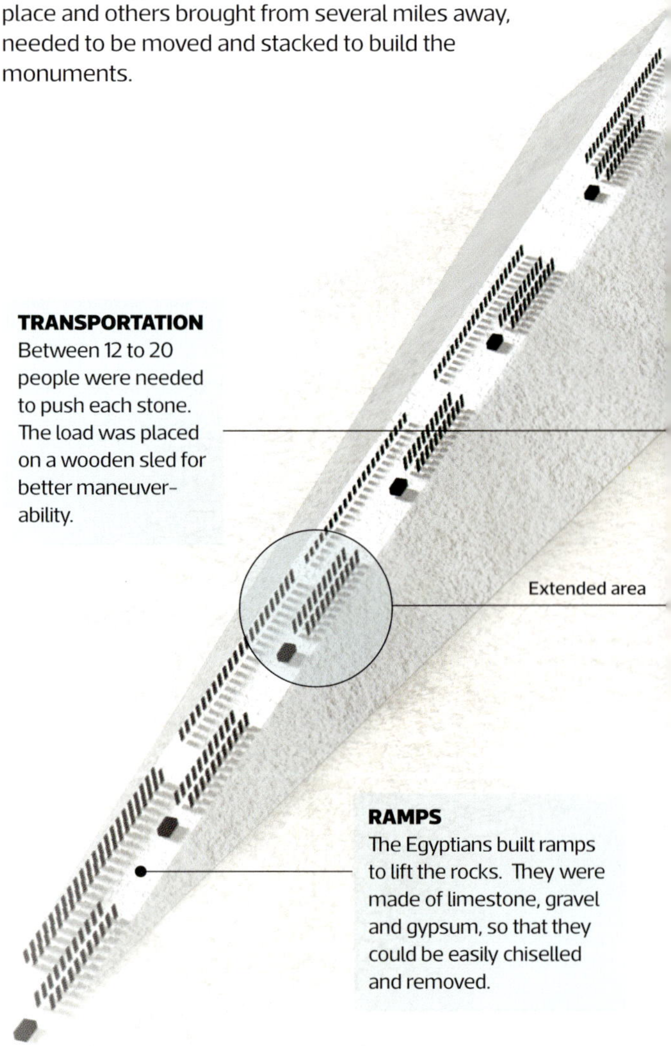

TRANSPORTATION
Between 12 to 20 people were needed to push each stone. The load was placed on a wooden sled for better maneuver-ability.

RAMPS
The Egyptians built ramps to lift the rocks. They were made of limestone, gravel and gypsum, so that they could be easily chiselled and removed.

Evolution

The side and spiral ramps were higher as the structure was completed. Upon completion, they were removed.

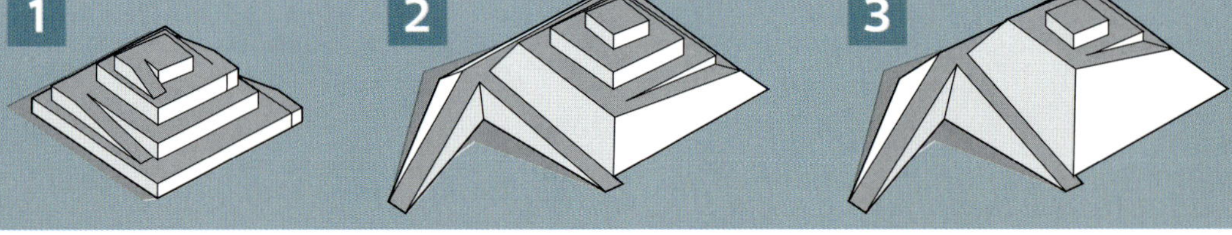

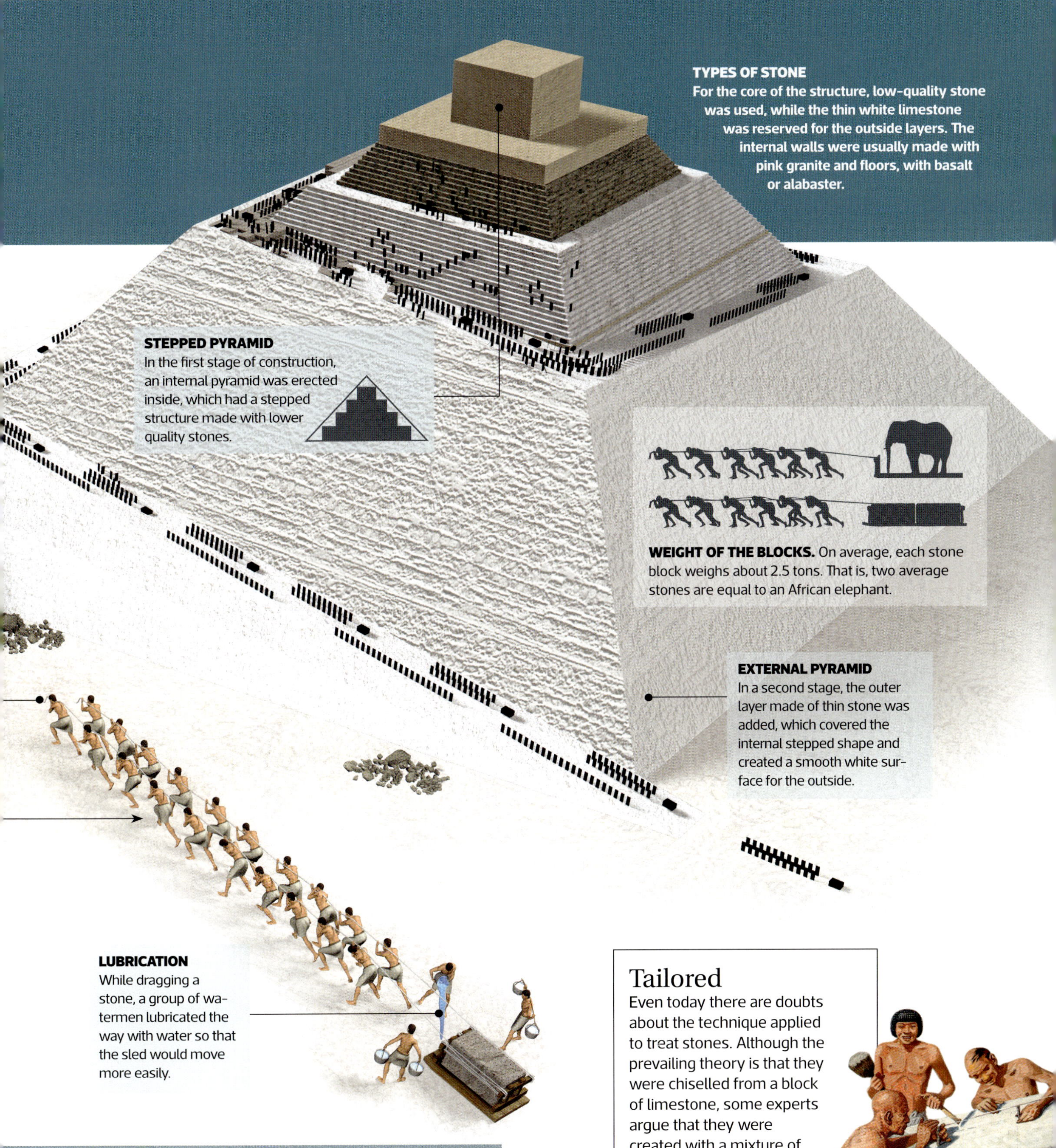

TYPES OF STONE
For the core of the structure, low-quality stone was used, while the thin white limestone was reserved for the outside layers. The internal walls were usually made with pink granite and floors, with basalt or alabaster.

STEPPED PYRAMID
In the first stage of construction, an internal pyramid was erected inside, which had a stepped structure made with lower quality stones.

WEIGHT OF THE BLOCKS. On average, each stone block weighs about 2.5 tons. That is, two average stones are equal to an African elephant.

EXTERNAL PYRAMID
In a second stage, the outer layer made of thin stone was added, which covered the internal stepped shape and created a smooth white surface for the outside.

LUBRICATION
While dragging a stone, a group of watermen lubricated the way with water so that the sled would move more easily.

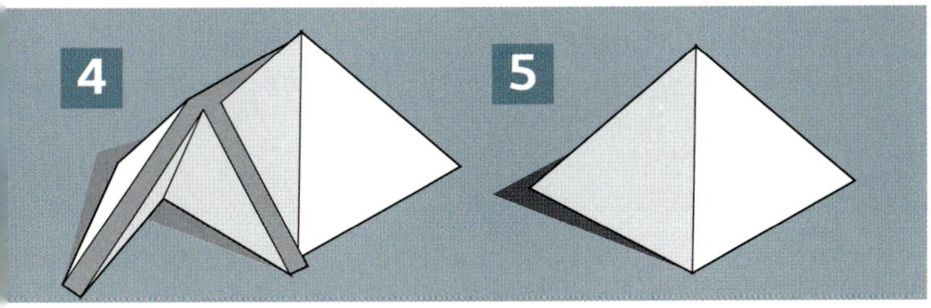

Tailored

Even today there are doubts about the technique applied to treat stones. Although the prevailing theory is that they were chiselled from a block of limestone, some experts argue that they were created with a mixture of limestone, clay, lime and water.

The Death of Tutankhamun

The first medical examinations made to the Pharaoh's mummy, through autopsy and radiography, shed some light on his life and death. The 2005 tomography clarified the remaining doubts and dismissed the murder theory.

Murder or Illness

It was never clear how Pharaoh Tutankhamun died, and the serious damage caused to the mummy when his bandages were removed in 1925 did not help to clarify the enigma. In 1968, Ronald G. Harrison, anatomist at the University of Liverpool, performed a radiography of the Pharaoh in his own tomb. He found a bone fragment and a dark spot on the skull, which fueled the murder theory, ruled out by a tomography done in 2005. Finally, DNA studies published in 2010 showed that the young king had a bone disease and had suffered from malaria, a combination that proved fatal.

Damage to the Skull

Tomographic studies performed in 2005 confirmed the presence of small fractures to the skull, but the experts dismissed that they had been caused during the life of Pharaoh. They attributed the damage to the embalmers and to the team of Howard Carter, discoverer of the tomb.

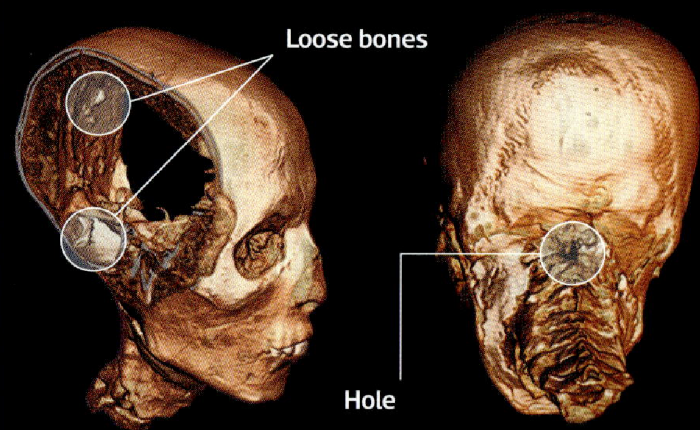

The Fracture of the Femur

The tomography revealed that the mummy had a fracture in the lower left femur. Some scientists believed that it was due to the embalmers or by Carter's team when he took the mummy from the sarcophagus. Others saw it as the cause of death of the Pharaoh (a poorly healed wound which became infected and led to his early death).

ZAHI HAWASS
This famous Egyptologist directed the CT scan that was performed on the mummy of Tutankhamun in 2005.

ACCIDENT?
This fracture in the femur of the Pharaoh led to think that maybe he had suffered a hunting accident that caused his death.

STRANGE RADIATION
Swiss geobiologist Blanche Merz measured a highly positive radiation in the uraeus (upright cobra) crowning the golden mask of Tutankhamun.

The Curse of Tutankhamun

The discovery of the tomb of the Pharaoh unleashed a storm of bad omens. It was said that the Defilers would be punished for their sacrilege. The string of deaths in future years, including that of Lord Carnarvon who financed and accompanied Carter at the opening of the tomb, fed the story of the curse, which was magnified by the press.

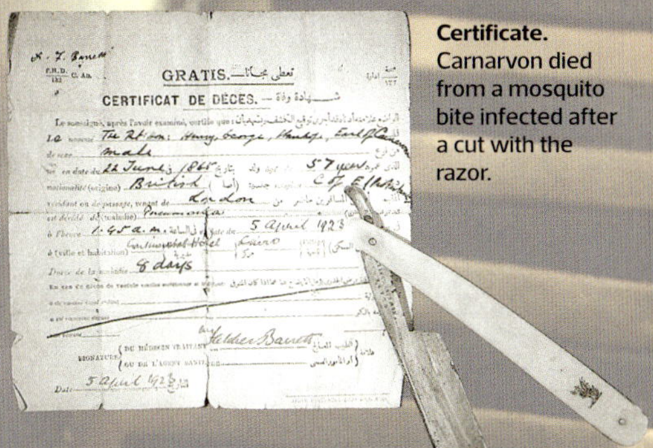

Certificate. Carnarvon died from a mosquito bite infected after a cut with the razor.

The Great Flood

The great weather catastrophe quoted by the Bible is at issue. Most experts believe it is a myth created by the oral tradition of ancient civilizations, but traces of natural disasters from the same time have been found.

Major Flooding

According to biblical calculations, the Flood could have occurred between 2360 and 2320 BC in the area of Mesopotamia, where the Euphrates and Tigris rivers draw nearer. In 1998, geologists William Ryan and Walter Pitman found there evidence of a massive flood, but dated a thousand years before the biblical disaster. Some experts argue that those floods, earlier snow-melt and frequent tropical rains, probably created the Flood myth in the collective memory as the great annihilating catastrophe reflected in the Old Testament.

DIVINE PUNISHMENT
The Genesis explains that the Flood was a divine punishment, which only Noah and his family survived aboard an ark with animals and seeds to repopulate the world.

1. Fertile Crescent. This valley would have been flooded after 40 days of continuous rain.

2. Mount Ararat. The Ark would have arrived here after 120 days adrift.

Biblical Geography

Most places and biblical events, such as the Flood, are located in the Middle East. Between the alleged flood area and Mount Ararat (Turkey) where the boat would have been stranded as the water level dropped down, in accordance with the Old Testament–there are more than 700 kilometers.

Mount Ararat

The Bible and History

1 4004 BC
According to the Ussher chronology, Creation and Eden coincide in time with the Mesopotamian Neolithic

2 2350 BC
The Flood could have occurred at the time that Sargon I began the conquests that led to the creation of the

3 1440-1295 BC
The Exodus narrated by the Bible may have taken place in the time frame between the reigns of Amenhotep II

4 950 BC
At the time of the biblical King Solomon of Israel, the Greeks colonized Asia Minor and the Assyrians conquered

Did the Ark of Noah Exist?

Until today there are only conjectures. In 1916, Russian explorer Vladimir Rosskowizky was the first to ensure that Mount Ararat, at 4,000 m in height, had a boat buried under the ice, but recent infra-red satellite photographs have been unable to confirm it.

DIMENSIONS
According to the Bible, the ark was about 135 m long and 23 wide, dimensions comparable to those of a large freighter today.

Dove Sent Forth from the Ark. Engraving by Gustave Doré, representing Noah's Ark on Mount Ararat.

The Ark of the Covenant

According to the Bible, the Ark of the Covenant is a tangible and sacred object. The Tablets of Law received by Moses on Mount Sinai, symbol of the pact between Yahweh and the Jewish people, were kept in it. Since 2500, its whereabouts have been unknown.

Where Is it Hidden?

In 586 BC, King Nebuchadnezzar II conquered Jerusalem and destroyed the Temple of Solomon and the sacred objects it housed, including the Ark. However, tradition leaves open the door to hope. The Bible says that Jeremiah had time to hide it on Mount Nebo and there is also the theory that it was stolen from the Temple by Menelik I, son of King Solomon, and taken to Axum, Ethiopia's Jerusalem.

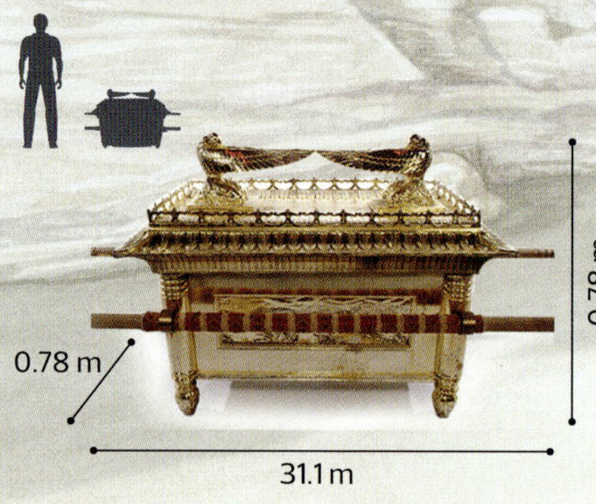

TECHNICAL SHEET

- **Main candidate:** Ark of the Church of Our Lady Mary of Zion in Axum (Ethiopia).
- **Biblical reference:** mentioned in the Old Testament, in Exodus (25: 10-21) and Samuel (6: 1).
- **Description:** Its construction was ordered by Moses according to the ordinances of Yahweh to house the Tablets of Law.
- **Weight:** it is believed to weigh from 90 kg up to 3.5 tons.

JEWISH FETISH
The Ark led the march of the people and the army, and its passing was announced by the sound of a ritual horn (shofar).

Leading the People

The Ark accompanied the Jewish people in its 40 years of exile, until their arrival at Palestine. It was also brought to the battles, and its power (according to the Bible) was such that it could defeat armies by its sole presence.

Safe in Ethiopia?

The Ethiopian Coptic Church, within Orthodox Christianity, states that the Ark of the Covenant is kept inside the Church of Our Lady Mary of Zion in Axum, (Ethiopia). Only a priest can see the Ark, which prevents attesting to the veracity of this claim by the Coptic Church.

SACRED JEWEL
Built with acacia wood, it was overlaid with gold and had two cherubim on top. In addition to the Tablets of Law, the Ark kept the budded staff of Aaron and a glass of manna.

REPLICA
Careful reproduction of the Ark in a room of the George Washington Masonic National Memorial, in Virginia. The Ark bears a strong symbolism to the Masons for their relationship with the Temple of Solomon.

REVERENTIAL ATTITUDE
During transportation, the Ark was wrapped in a blue cloth. It remained hidden even to those who transported it. They could not touch it. Therefore, rods were used to move it.

The Quest for the Holy Grail

The Holy Grail is one of the most important European myths of the Middle Ages, with Christian, Celtic and Oriental roots. Was it really the chalice used by Jesus at the Last Supper? Was a simple relic or the source of an almost divine power?

The Enduring Legend

The myth begins with the arrival of Joseph of Arimathea to Glastonbury, on the English coast, where he built the first church in Britain. It guarded the chalice with which, according to tradition, he had collected the blood of Jesus on the cross. From this history, many legends arose about healing and rejuvenating powers of the relic and its true whereabouts. According to the Catholic Church, it is "absolutely plausible" that the Holy Grail is the little agate cup that in the 15th century came to the Saint Mary's Cathedral in Valencia (Spain).

DATA SHEET

- **Main candidate:** Holy Chalice of Valencia (Spain).
- **Biblical reference:** it is mentioned in the Gospels of Matthew (26: 26-29), Mark (14: 22-25), Luke (22: 15-20) and First Corinthians (11: 23-27)
- **Description:** The name of a legendary sacred vessel, identified also as the Eucharist chalice used by Jesus at the Last Supper.
- **Weight:** no data.

Why Did the Nazis Covet the Grail?

Influenced by the neo-paganism that emerged in the first third of the 20th century, the leaders of the Nazi Party wanted to create a mythology of their own and were interested in integrating the Holy Grail in their doctrine. Their quest intended to legitimize the Aryan race as the true heir of Christ. The Nazi leader who was more involved in the task was Heinrich Himmler, head of the SS. He first commissioned the Grail quest to medievalist Otto Rahn, who inquired in France, and then to Colonel Otto Skorzeny, with no results in both cases.

Heinrich Himmler. Fervent follower of the occult beliefs, he unsuccessfully sought the Holy Grail.

The crypt of the SS. Himmler built a temple for Aryan culture in Wewelsburg Castle (Germany). In this round Crypt, he reserved an empty and preferential place for the Grail.

LEGENDARY CHALICE
Perceval holding the Holy Grail in this illustration from the late 13th century.

The Figure of Perceval

From the 12th century, various medieval romances recount the adventures of Perceval, one of the knights of the Round Table, who got to see the Grail in a castle of Montsalvat mountain, inhabited by the Fisher King. The figure of Perceval links the Grail tradition with the famous literary cycle dedicated to King Arthur. In the Arthurian legends, finding the Holy Grail, which had supernatural properties, was conceived as an allegory of spiritual enlightenment.

The Writings of the Dead Sea

Their discovery has shed new light on Judaism and early Christianity, but since its finding was made public, in 1947, they have been the subject of much controversy. Who wrote them? What secrets do they still keep?

Handwritten Testimony

In late 1946, a Bedouin shepherd incidentally came across a cave located in the mountains of Qumran, near the Dead Sea. He found several jars containing mysterious handwritten scrolls in it, mainly in Hebrew and Aramaic. After passing through the hands of different merchants, the parchments were authenticated and dated, and that led to search for more caves and manuscripts in the area. It is believed that the texts, the oldest of their kind, were hidden by the Jewish community in the caves before the destruction of Qumran by the Romans around the year 68 BC.

THE CAVES
The scrolls were found scattered in 11 caves at Qumran. Between 1951 and 1963, more manuscripts were found nearby, which are also considered Dead Sea Scrolls.

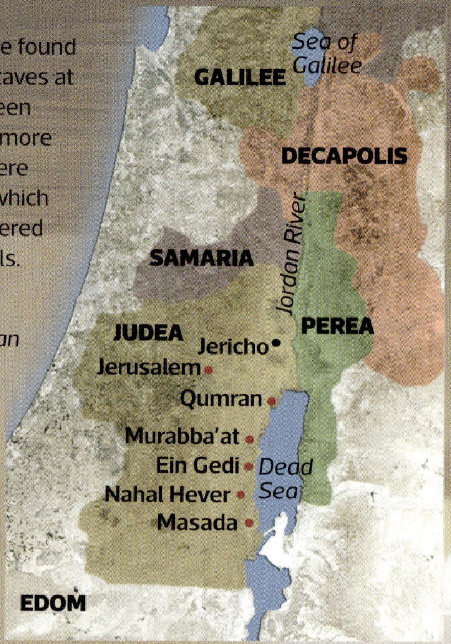

• Location of Manuscripts

The Mystery of Papyrus 7Q5

Some experts have identified the manuscript 7Q5, dated between 50 BC and 50 AD, as a text from the *Gospel of Mark*. If the hypothesis were true, it would mean that the Gospel is closer to the historical Jesus than it was believed.

Papyrus 7Q5. The controversial 7Q5 fragment, written in Greek, is a small irregular piece of just 3.9 x 2.7 cm.

THE COPYISTS
The scribes copied texts in the scrolls under the vigilance of supervisors.

BOOK OF ISAIAH
This long manuscript was the first to be found (in Cave 1), and it is the best preserved.

Qumran Scriptorium

In the ruins of the archaeological site of Qumran, a long hall is highlighted known as *scriptorium* (the writing room), where allegedly some of the texts found in the nearby caves were copied. Benches and tables, in addition to inkwells and jars similar to those of the caves, were also found, which would prove the link between the citadel and the caves.

The Treasure of the Copper Scroll

In 1952 a special scroll was found in Cave 3 at Qumran. It is not made with a parchment or a papyrus, but with copper, and the location of 64 places in Israel where great wealth was hidden was inscribed on its two plates. Although it lacks precise indications, archaeologists and treasure hunters still seek the spoils.

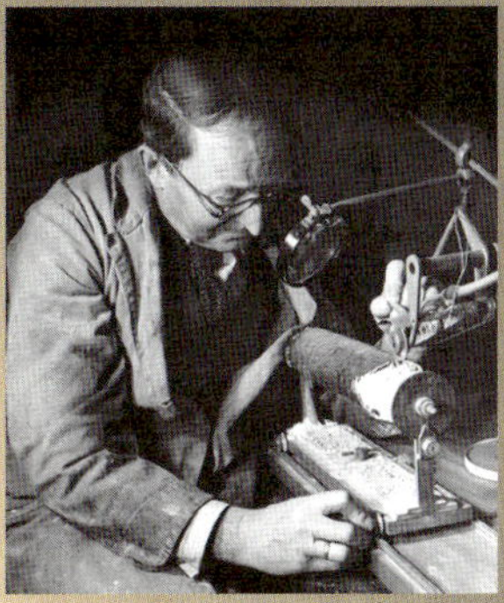

Wright Bake. Professor Baker at the historic moment when he opened the Copper Scroll in 1956.

DICTATION
A community member dictates a sacred text to a copyist. The scrolls had to be made of "pure" animals and its preparation was done according to specific rules of hygiene.

QUMRAN BENCHES
The tables and benches in this room (second floor of locus 30, by designation of the archaeologists) are indicative of its use as a *scriptorium*.

***Scriptorium* at Qumran.** Recreation of the room where some Dead Sea Scrolls were possibly written.

The Secret Life of Jesus

The Gospels do not explain everything. Other early writings outside the canon of the Catholic Church, the so-called apocryphal gospels, fill the gaps with the image of a more human Jesus, capable of falling in love and hating. Perhaps closer to the truth?

Parallel Stories

Given that ancient texts are always a product of their time, their context and the intentions of those who wrote them, it stands to reason that the real Jesus was not exactly like the one described in the Gospels. Thus, in 1945 a clay pot was found at Nag Hammadi (Egypt) with documents on the life of Jesus, the age of which was tested with carbon-14, speaking of a very human character, he felt passions such as love, hate and anger.

Did he Travel to the Himalayas?

The Gospels are silent on the life of Jesus between his 12 and 30 years of age. What did he do during those "missing years"? Some defend the theory that, before starting his preaching, Jesus travelled to India and the Himalayas.

Travel Initiation In the Himalayas, Jesus acquired the knowledge that enabled him to build his philosophy.

Another Ending

Many Christians asked themselves why the Son of God accepted such a cruel and humiliating death. Therefore, there have always been speculations that he did not die on the cross. According to Basilides, a Gnostic Egyptian, Jesus was replaced by Simon of Cyrene, the person who helped him carry the cross.

Under the Weight of the Cross. Oil painting by Caravaggio in which Jesus is helped by Simon of Cyrene.

EGYPT

Main Stages of Jesus' Journey

1 Bethlehem
Birth and early days in Jesus' life. Tradition says that Herod the Great ordered to kill all the children born in Bethlehem under two years of age to prevent them from dethroning him as King of the Jews.

2 Egypt
According to the Gospel of Matthew (2, 13-15), an angel appeared in a dream of Joseph and said to him: "Get up, take the child and his mother and escape to Egypt." The family remained there until the death of King Herod.

3 Nazareth
Mary, Joseph and Jesus settled in the city of Nazareth when returning from Egypt to fulfil the prophecy of the Old Testament: "The Savior will be called a Nazarene." Herod Antipas ruled in Galilee.

4 Jerusalem
There are two major events of Jesus in Jerusalem: at age 12, when he discussed with the wise men in the Temple, and at 33, when he entered the city riding on a donkey, shortly before he was crucified on Mount Calvary.

THE WORLD OF THE MESSIAH
Judea and Galilee, in the Middle East, were the alleged preaching areas of Jesus, although some believe he reached India.

5 India
There are researchers who believe that Jesus travelled to India with some merchants when he was 12 or 13 years old, and lived there before returning to Palestine. For some, his actual grave is in Kashmir.

6 Qasr el Yahud
In this place along the Jordan River was where John baptized Jesus, marking the beginning of his public life. It is not known if it occurred on the western shore, current territory of Israel, or the eastern one, current Jordan.

7 Capernaum
Located along the Sea of Galilee, this was the town where Jesus, after spending 40 days in the desert, began his preaching and carried out his first miraculous healing. It is mentioned in the Gospel of Mark.

8 Canaan
According to the Gospel of John, the first miracle of Jesus took place here: turning water into wine at a wedding. Apocrypha argue that was the ceremony of his marriage with Mary Magdalene.

9 Mount Tabor
In this place, the Transfiguration of Jesus in front of the apostles Peter, John and James took place. The Son of God changed his appearance and the prophets Moses and Elijah, who had passed long before, appeared next to him.

The Gospel of Judas

Did Christianity usurp the true teachings of Jesus? A codex that remained hidden in the desert sands for nearly two millennia puts into question many of the conventions on the origin of this religion.

The Codex Tchacos

Dated between 220-340 AD, this papyrus codex found in 1978 near El Minya (Egypt) contains four Gnostic texts, among which is the controversial *Gospel of Judas* (occupying pages 33-58). With a complex translation, this text seems to question one of the basic beliefs of Christianity: the betrayal of Judas Iscariot to Jesus the night of the Last Supper.

The Controversial Text

The story is attributed to Judas Iscariot, the traitor who turned Jesus in. The text narrates the Passion of Christ in a heretic way and features a heroic Judas as Jesus' favorite disciple. It is estimated that the original text was written by early Christian Gnostics.

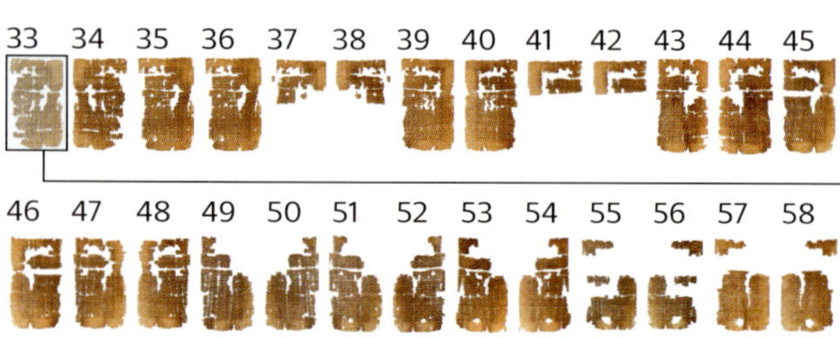

Heretical Gospel

Around 180 AD, Bishop Irenaeus of Lyons wrote his famous work *Against Heresies*, by which he established the four Gospels that were considered canonical by the Church (Matthew, Mark, Luke and John) and situated the *Gospel of Judas* among heretical texts.

FIRST PAGE
The text begins: "The secret account of the revelation that Jesus spoke in conversation with Judas Iscariot during eight days, three days before he celebrated Passover (...)."

Hero or Traitor?

Even before the appearance of the *Gospel of Judas*, there were those who wondered if Judas behavior was reprehensible, since it was part of God's holy plan. Without him, the crucifixion and resurrection would not have occurred.

Kiss of Judas. The episode of treason in the famous painting by Giotto.

The "30 Coins"

There are texts that consider that the amount received by Judas to betray Jesus was insignificant (in order to humiliate the Master), and others, however, say that you could buy a farm field with that money.

THE CONDITION OF THE CODEX
The codex, protected by leather wrapping, was kept in good condition thanks to the low humidity of the Egyptian desert. But after its discovery, it was kept in a safe box in New York for 16 years, where it suffered great deterioration.

WRITING
The ink used is a composition of ferrous sulfate, tannin, gum arabic and water, mixed with carbon black dye.

Who Wrote the Gospel of Judas?

The author or authors of the text remain anonymous, but they certainly belong to a branch of Gnosticism. Therefore, the Codex Tchacos would have been written in a region of Gnostic activity (Alexandria, Syria or Asia Minor), and it would have been sent a from there to a community in Middle Egypt.

The Sacred Shroud

The Shroud of Turin is considered one of the most important relics of Christianity. For those who believe in it, this is the sheet that covered the body of Jesus Christ after his crucifixion. For sceptics, it's just a fake.

The Marks of the Shroud

Whether it is fake or not, the Shroud has a number of marks of different origin and different times, which have been analyzed and identified in depth. The marks left on the cloth, however, remain controversial for researchers.

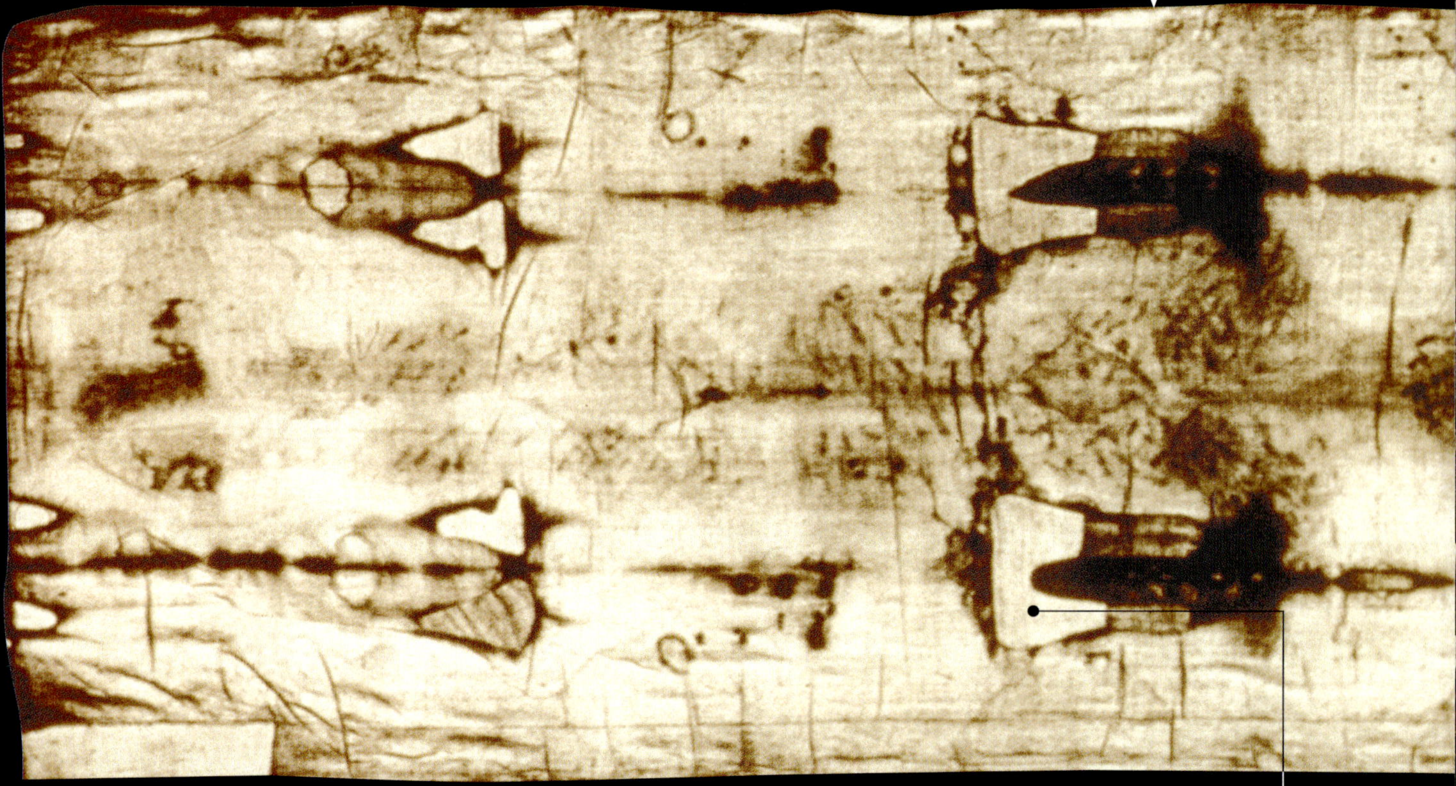

BURNS AND PATCHES
In 1532, a drop of silver molten during a fire burned a corner of the Shroud (which was folded), leaving several triangular holes. Two years later, patches were applied on the holes.

How did it Arrive at Turin?

Some scholars identify the Shroud with the *Mandylion*, or Image of Edessa (Turkey). From there, it reached Constantinople and then its track was lost after the sacking of the Fourth Crusade. In 1355, it "reappeared" in Lirey, a small town in France. Finally, in 1578, the Duke of Savoy decided its final transfer to Turin, to the Cathedral of Saint John the Baptist.

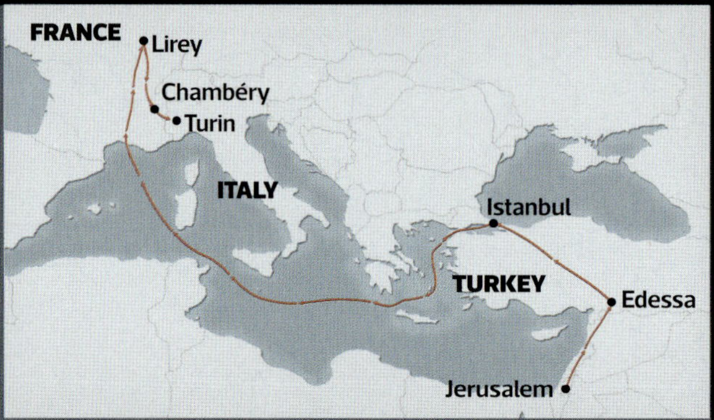

EXPOSITORY PREACHING
Promotional poster for the Expository Preaching of 1898, during which the first photographies of the Shroud were obtained, which attracted world-wide interest.

Model or Copy?

Scholars have highlighted the similarities between medieval icons of Christ Pantocrator and the Shroud face. They have pointed up to 15 matches (cheekbones, eyes, beard, etc.). Sceptics, however, believe that the influence has been reversed, from the icons to the Canvas.

THE FACE
The face is swollen, as if it were a result of the blows suffered.

BLOOD WOUNDS
There are signs of a significant blood flow on the left side of the body, where Christ received a spear on the cross in accordance with tradition. The stain spreads through the back of the canvas.

TRAIL OF NAILS
The arms are outstretched, with his hands crossed above his body. A smear of blood on the wrist caused by iron nail penetration can be clearly noticed.

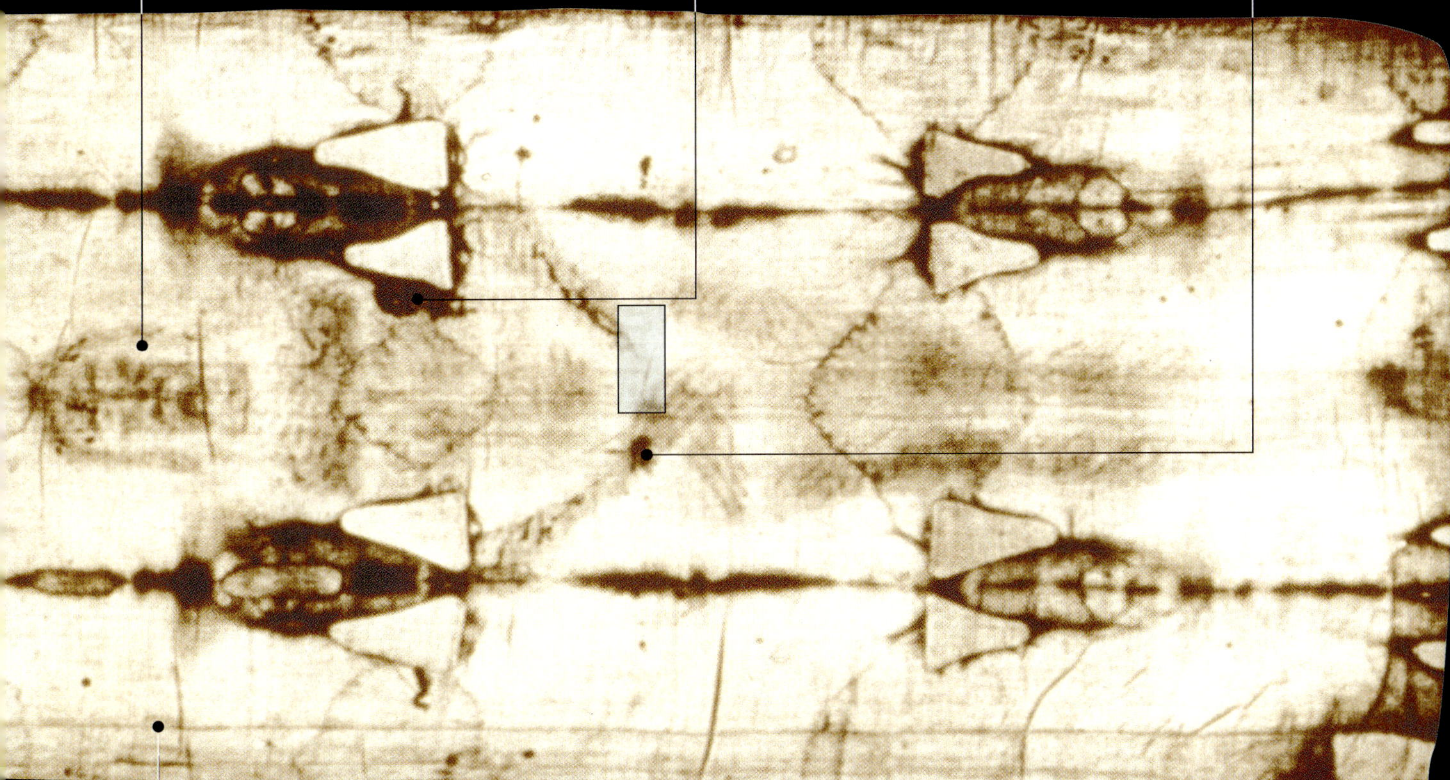

THIN STRIP
According to some scholars, the thin strip of the lower edge of the Canvas is a later addition. It still forms part of the relic, unlike the triangular patches added in 1534, which were removed in 2002.

The STURP Project

In 1978, a group of 33 scientists was created to study the cloth. It was denominated the STURP project. Three years later, the team presented its final report, concluding that the bloodstains were real. But there was one dissenting voice: chemist Walter McCrone said there were traces of ochre and vermilion paint, suggesting that it was a fake.

Chapter 2

Enigmas of the Middle Age and Modern Times

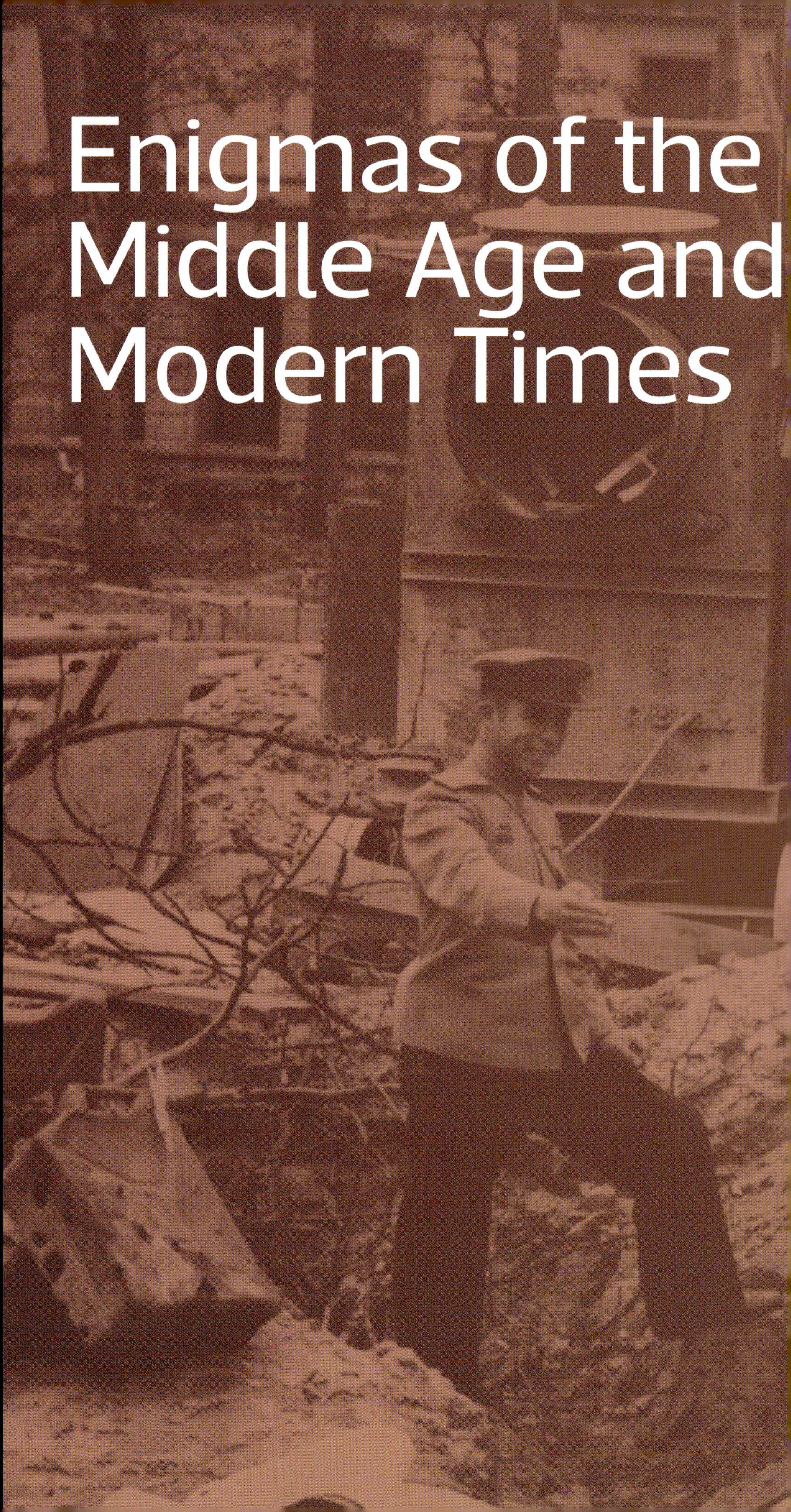

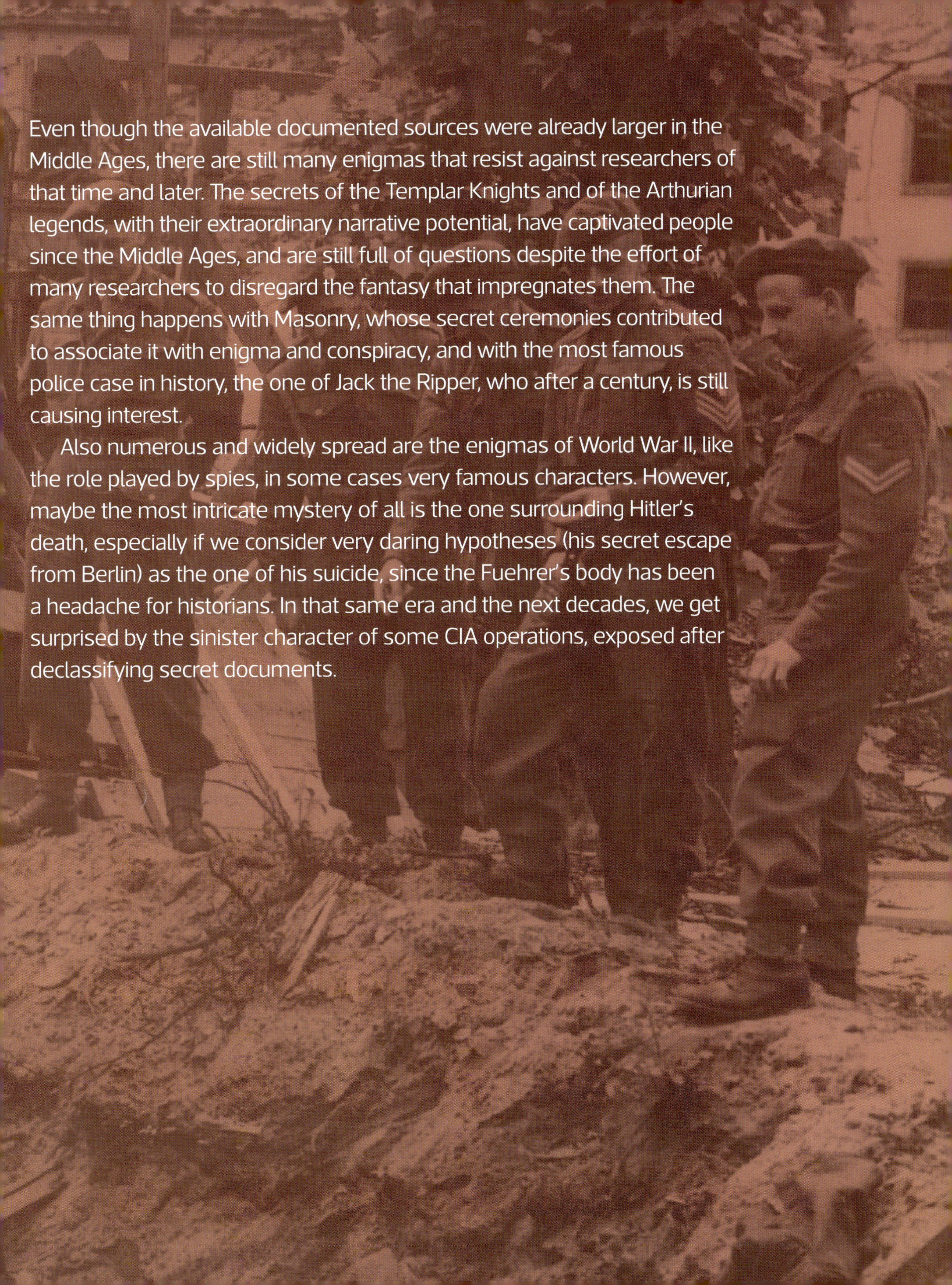

Even though the available documented sources were already larger in the Middle Ages, there are still many enigmas that resist against researchers of that time and later. The secrets of the Templar Knights and of the Arthurian legends, with their extraordinary narrative potential, have captivated people since the Middle Ages, and are still full of questions despite the effort of many researchers to disregard the fantasy that impregnates them. The same thing happens with Masonry, whose secret ceremonies contributed to associate it with enigma and conspiracy, and with the most famous police case in history, the one of Jack the Ripper, who after a century, is still causing interest.

Also numerous and widely spread are the enigmas of World War II, like the role played by spies, in some cases very famous characters. However, maybe the most intricate mystery of all is the one surrounding Hitler's death, especially if we consider very daring hypotheses (his secret escape from Berlin) as the one of his suicide, since the Fuehrer's body has been a headache for historians. In that same era and the next decades, we get surprised by the sinister character of some CIA operations, exposed after declassifying secret documents.

The Myth of King Arthur

Few historical enigmas have retained their power to fascinate people throughout the centuries like the one of Arthur. The scarce documentation about the existence of this Celtic king did not decrease its influence on European culture.

Son of the Legend

Well known historians consider that maybe around the 5th or 6th centuries, a character named Artorius existed, of Roman origin and who fought with the Britons against the invaders from the continent. But some time later, many local legends have been attributed to that leader. The ability of Geoffrey de Monmouth and other Arthurian authors was the presentation, as an historical tale, of what was pure invention.

MORDRED
Arthur's incestuous son. He is the traitor of the legend. Skilled manipulator, he took the Court to the ruin.

LANCELOT
Son of king Ban de Benoic, adopted by the Lady in the Lake, he incarnates the strength and weakness of the Round Table.

BEDIVERE
Marshal of Logres and Arthur's companion. He was born in Normandy and was buried in Bayeux.

PERCIVAL
Main hero of the first novels of the Grail. He was known as "the perfect fool."

GAWAIN
The oldest of king Lot's sons. Lancelot's friend, in some versions he is mortally wounded by him.

Chronology of the main Arthurian stories

The main works that talk about king Arthur are presented as historical treaties. The others are cavalry novels.

830
Historia Brittonum
Nennius
It tells the early history of England and Wales. First mention of Arthur as a historical figure.

1138
Historia Regum Britanniae
Geoffrey of Monmouth
Pseudo historical work. Based on *Historia Brittonum*, among others. First mention of Excalibur sword.

1155
Roman de Brut
Wace
The Anglo-Norman poet writes about the origins of England in French. First mention of the Round table.

c.1170
Lancelot, the knight of the cart
Chretien de Troyes
This poem is the first mention of Lancelot and Camelot, king Arthur's Court.

1191
Percival, the Tale of the Grail
Chretien de Troyes
Ilnspired in Celtic traditions and British legends, it mentions the Holy Grail for the first time.

c.1200
Joseph of Arimathea. Merlin
Robert de Boron
The Grail takes an explicitly Christian value in these two poetic works.

The Round Table

The habitual image that presents the myth of the knights of the Round Table probably has not much to do with what could have been the Arthurian environment in the 5th and 6th centuries. The number of knights that sat around it varies according to different authors: from 12, the classics of Arthurian iconography, to even 1,600 guests.

PELLINORE
Arthur's loyal ally and king. After killing king Lot, his dynasty and the Round Table started to fail.

BORS
Son of king Bohort and Lionel's brother. He was the only knight that returned to Camelot after looking at the Grail.

TRISTAN
A historical figure whose tomb would be near Fowey. Nephew of king Mark of Cornwall.

LIONEL
Sir Bors' brother. He supported Lancelot against Arthur and was named king of Gaunnes.

GALAHAD
The noblest knight of the Round Table. Descendent of Joseph of Arimathea. Son of Lancelot and Elaine.

KEY
One of the first knights of Arthur. He is the seneschal of the kingdom and Arthur's adopted brother.

c.1210

Parzival
Wolfram von Eschenbach
It completes the unfinished work of Troyes, with new contributions about the origin of the Holy Grail.

1215/1235

Vulgate Cycle
Anonymous
Five works that present the first joined structure of the legend. Galahad is introduced.

1485

Le Morte d'Arthur
Thomas Malory
It recollects the different traditions of the Arthurian cycle. The most influential version in later periods.

The Legend of Merlin

Merlin's figure is almost equal in importance and fame as the one of the own King Arthur. Alchemist, druid and political advisor, he was one of the great Pan-European characters, and his magical figure has been subject of constant revisions for centuries.

Celtic Tradition

The historical base of the Merlin is double. On one side, it is a copy of Lailoken, a bard from the 6th century who became a madman when his king died in the Battle of Arfderydd. The Welsh version of this tradition had the leading role on bard Myrddin, who writer Geoffrey of Monmouth translated as Merlin, being the first one to use that name and defined the character. The second origin is located in the legend of Ambrose the Child, son of a princess and an evil spirit, who prophesied the final victory of the red dragon (Celts or Welsh) over the white dragon (Saxons).

CASTLE OF TINTAGEL
Located on the east coast of Cornwall (southeast of England), this castle overlooking the Atlantic Ocean was, according to tradition, the birthplace of King Arthur. On the lower part of the cliff there is a cave where, the legend says, Merlin used to live.

Merlin in the Arthurian World

The Welsh magician owes his fame, mainly, to his participation in the Arthurian legend, where he played a very important role as counselor of king Uther and his son Arthur. These are the main characters that appear in literary texts.

Arthur
During his youth he was recognized as a brilliant idealist and an infallible warrior. He was accepted as king thanks to Merlin

Guinevere
Daughter of King Leodegrance, married to King Arthur. Her infidelity with Lancelot brought the Round Table to a downfall

Uther Pendragon
King of Britain, in the legend he is Arthur's father; he seduces Lady Igraine after fighting against Gorlois at the castle of Dimilioc

Mordred
Arthur's incestuous son. He is the traitor of the legend; he corrupted King Arthur's Court as Merlin had foreseen

Morgan Le Fay
Arthur's sister, with which he had Mordred. In some narrations she is benevolent, and in others she is shown as against Arthur

Morgause
Arthur's sister too, she was married to king Lot, her brother's great enemy, and was the mother of knight Gawain

The End of the Magician

The legend says that, once in his old age, Merlin fell deeply in love with a young woman, the Lady of the Lake. In exchange for her love, he taught her all the secrets of his magic, including the spell to lock a man. The young woman was afraid of him and she used black magic to imprison him in a tree, a rock, or according to another version, in a glass cage.

THE LADY OF THE LAKE
Viviane (or Nimue in some tales), was the daughter of the king of Northumberland. She educated the knight Lancelot and seduced Merlin, from whom she stole his magic secrets.

Merlin and Stonehenge

For G. of Monmouth, Merlin was who, using his powers, moved the huge circle of stones from Ireland to Stonehenge to comply with the wishes of king Ambrosius Aurelianus. According to the legend, Uther Pendragon, Arthur's father, was buried there.

Excalibur

According to *Historia Regum Britanniae*, Merlin forged the famous sword in Avalon Island, and embedded it in a stone with an inscription: "This is the sword Excalibur. Whoever takes It out of this anvil, will be the king of England." Arthur was the chosen one.

The Treasure of the Templar

In the Order of the Temple there were bankers of kings, guardians of royal treasures, feudal landowners and important lords. However, during the process that ended up in the dissolution of this order, no traces of its fortune were found.

What Happened with the Riches of the Templar?

The treasure of the templar became a myth from the moment of their detention in 1307. Royal civil servants that took control of encomiendas, abbeys and castles of the Templar in France, Castile, Aragon and Portugal did not find great amounts of money or valuable relics. Even though the Templar were monks, and theoretically what they generated was destined to the fight in Holy Land, some people believe that the treasure existed and that it was hidden very well.

The Treasure of the Gisors

In 1946, Roger Lhomoy, guard of Gisors castle (in Normandy, France) claimed he had found an underground passage with statues, sarcophaguses and chests with precious metals: the famous treasure of the Templar. But the tunnel he had dug endangered a tower, and Lhomoy abandoned the digging.

Gisors. In 1964 new diggings were going to be done, but the place was declared a military zone and they were banned.

Financing of Cathedrals

A theory with not much endorsement claims that the Templar money could have been used to finance the Gothic cathedrals in France. The "proof" would be that these monuments started to be constructed after the fire (provoked?) of the previous temple during the functioning of the Order. That is the case of Tours (1176), Chartres (towards 1220) and Reims (1211). Some people see the hand of Bernard of Clairvaux, main ambassador of the Templar behind them.

BERNARD OF CLAIRVAUX
The good relationship between this French monk and Luis VII's advisor, abbot Suger (promoter of the change from Romanic to Gothic) has made believe that the cathedrals could have been financed with the money of the Templar.

Reims Cathedral.

HOW THEY AMASSED THEIR FORTUNE

The economic takeoff of the Order of the Templar arrived after the success of the propaganda that lead to the Council of Troyes (1129), with the increase of donations from noblemen and bourgeoisie of Christian Europe.

Out of France

Some people claim that the Templar could have taken their treasure out of Paris, getting ahead of Phillip IV's action. Researchers like Stephen Defoe and Alan Butler say that it ended being hidden in Switzerland, where the Templar turned small rural communities in what today is the most famous and most secret banking society in the world.

The Masonic Lodges

Even though they have been exerting a notable influence on all the world and generating very radical opinions in favor and against for three centuries, Masons are still a mystery. The complexity of Masonry has favored its enigmatic halo.

A Power in the Shadows?

Many world leaders have belonged to Masonry, which today gathers more than five million people In the world. It is said that Masons had influence on the French Revolution, The Independence of America, and that they infiltrated in the Vatican, although there are no definite proofs of any of these cases.

The Maximum Symbol. It is the Great Architect of the Universe: a compass, a set-square and the G of Gnosis.

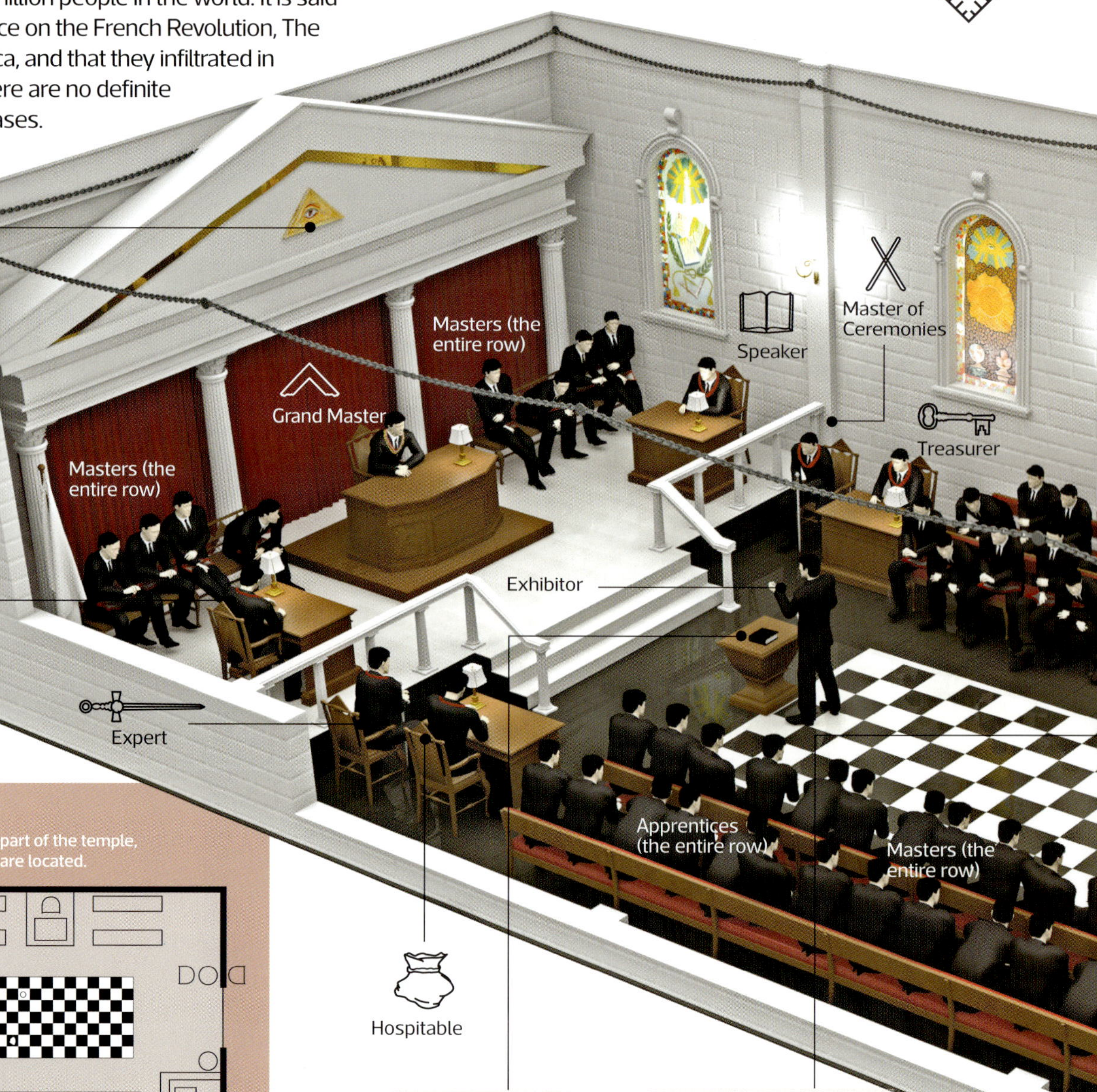

THE ALL-SEEING EYE
It represents, in some way, self consciousness.

PLACE OF HONOR
Where the book of Sacred Law is placed, along with a compass and a square.

THE THREE COLUMNS
They represent beauty, strength and wisdom, which are Masonry's objectives.

THE SECTORS

Orient. It is the most elevated part of the temple, where the highest authorities are located.

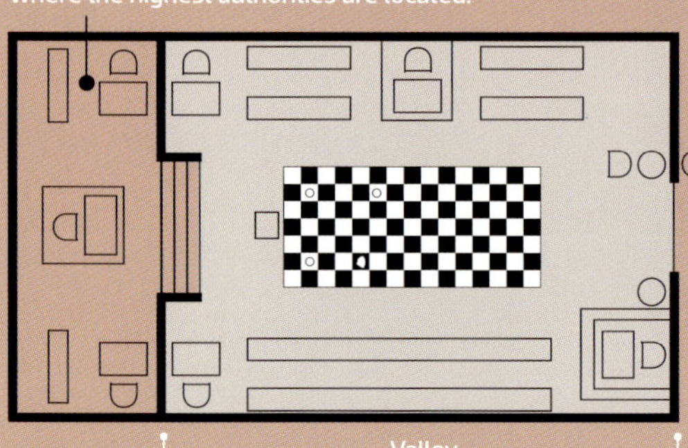

Apprentices and fellows are located here, along with the authorities.

Were they Masons? From left to right, Wolfgang A. Mozart, Isaac Newton and Voltaire.

Famous Personalities

Secrecy of the lodges, together with anti Masonry propaganda from the Church and anti liberal sectors, pushed many masons to hide their affiliation. But it is well known that Mozart, Voltaire or George Washington belonged to lodges, while there is no documented evidence for cases like the ones of Newton or Napoleon.

The Temple and its Symbols

The Lodges or Masonic temples are thought as a representation of the Universe. It can be said that each piece of furniture, each inscription and ornamentation in dressing, and each gesture of the participants in the meetings has a meaning. In the inside of these temples, oriented to the East, order and symbolisms stand out.

PILLARS
There are two, the Boaz and the Jakim, both topped by a globe and a grenade that represent universality and fraternal union.

In Daily Life

Experts claim that the world Is full of buildings, objects, marks and emblems that contain Masonic symbols. Proof of that are one dollar bills, with multiple mentions of number 13, figure that symbolizes transformation for masons.

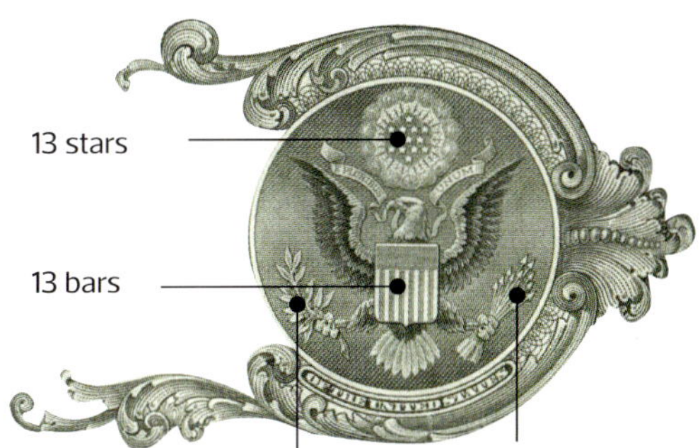

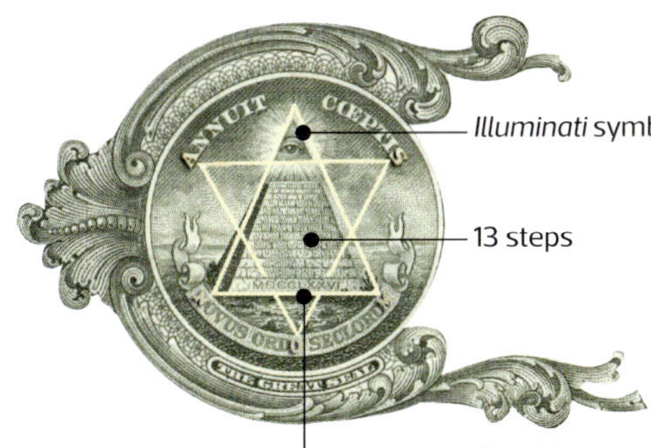

STAR OF DAVID
The star can be traced on the pyramid of the bill, joining the letters A in Annuit, S in Coeptis, N In Novus, O in Ordo and M in Seclorum. In order they form the word "MASON."

The Rosicrucian and the *Illuminati*

In the 17th and 18th centuries, some secret societies with an esoteric character appeared, closely related with Masonry like the Rosicrucian and the *Illuminati*, who tried to influence the way of thinking and governing the world.

The Order of the Rosy Cross

Born in the 17th century and heir of the esoteric order founded by German traveler of the 14th century Christian Rosenkreutz (allegorical name whose identity - and even his existence - is still discussed), the Rosicrucian used parascientific disciplines (alchemy, Jewish Cabbala, Hermeticism) to achieve inner piece. Spread throughout Latin America from a "refoundation" in the 19th century, this secret society is divided in various organizations. The most numerous one is the Ancient and Mystic Order of the Rosy Cross.

THE PELICAN, THE ROSE AND THE CROSS
They are the main symbols of the Order of the Rosicrucian, created under protestant inspiration as a counterpoint to the Company of Jesus.

HERMETIC ORDER OF THE GOLDEN DAWN
Descendent of the German Rosicrucian, this secret society dedicated to ceremonial magic and occultism was founded in London in 1888 by William Wynn Westcott and Samuel MacGregor Mathers.

SYMBOL
The truncated pyramid and the Eye that sees all, together with the motto *Novus Ordo Seclorum* are considered a symbol of the *Illuminati*.

The Enlightened from Bavaria

The *Illuminati* are a secret society founded in 1776 with the purpose of overthrowing governments and kingdoms, eliminate religions and private property, and create what they called a New World Order, expression that appears in one dollar bills and that has been repeated so many times by American presidents. It is supposed that currently the *Illuminati* still exist and are working to favor globalization.

Owl of Minerva. This bird associated to the goddess of wisdom is another one of the symbols of the *Illuminati*.

Temple. Allegorical representation of the Rosicrucian.

College of the Invisibles

In the 17th century, a group of Rosicrucian led by important scientists such as Robert Hooke and Robert Boyle, and by architect Christopher Wren, founded in London what was called College of the Invisibles, a secret society for reflection about philosophy, science and alchemy, which received support from king Charles II of England to become the Royal Society, origin of the modern Masonry.

Masons and Rosicrucian

There has always been a controversy between both organizations and have even been mixed up. While Masons claim that Rosicrucian were inspired in their organization (they called their meeting places lodges, they established a similar hierarchical order and also use the apron as a symbolic garment), Rosicrucian claim that Masonry is a split of the Order of Rosy Cross, and remind us that the main Masonic rites call "Sovereign Rosicrucian Prince" one of the degrees In the brotherhood, nomenclature that prove its influence.

DEGREE 18
It is the place that the Sovereign Rosicrucian Prince occupies in the scale of degrees of the Mason Scottish Rite. In the French Rite, it is located on the seventh and last degree.

Scottish Rite

This Masonic rite, very common in Europe and Latin America, is made by 33 degrees. The first three degrees (Apprentice, Fellow and Master) are the base of Universal symbolic Masonry.

Vlad Draculea, the Impaler

This sinister character that Bram Stoker used as reference for his famous novel *Dracula* lived in the 15th century. He ruled the principality of Wallachia (on the border with Transylvania), and entered history for his cruelty, slaughters and his passion for blood.

Was Vlad a Vampire?

German legends from the 16th century describe Vlad Draculea as a barbarian and a tyrant, but they never attributed him the features of a vampire. It would not be until 1897, with the publishing of *Dracula* by Irish Bram Stoker, when prince Vlad was associated with these bloodthirsty beings. Due to his history and for the evocative power of his name: Draculea not only means "son of the Dragon" but also "son of the Devil." Also, there were legends about vampires in the neighbor Transylvania (then a part of Hungary), so everything fit in for the vampire myth to take shape.

THE CREATOR
Bram Stoker gave the most notable of the vampires a bond with the historical character Vlad Draculea.

EAST EUROPE IN 1450

Wallachia in the 15th Century

The principality of Vlad the Impaler spread from the south of the Carpathian Mountains to the shores of the Danube River, and from the Siret River, to the east, to the narrow gorge of the Danube(known as the Iron Doors), to the west. Half a million Wallachians used to live in this plain, in small and poorly defended cities.

POENARI CASTLE
This inaccessible fortress over the Arges River was Vlad's residence, and not Bran's castle, which appears in *Dracula*.

The nailed turbans

Vlad Draculea was implacable in front of anyone who questioned him. It is said that when he received a delegation from sultan Mehmed II, he asked the Turkish emissaries to uncover their heads in front of him and, after their refusal; he ordered to have their turbans nailed to their skulls.

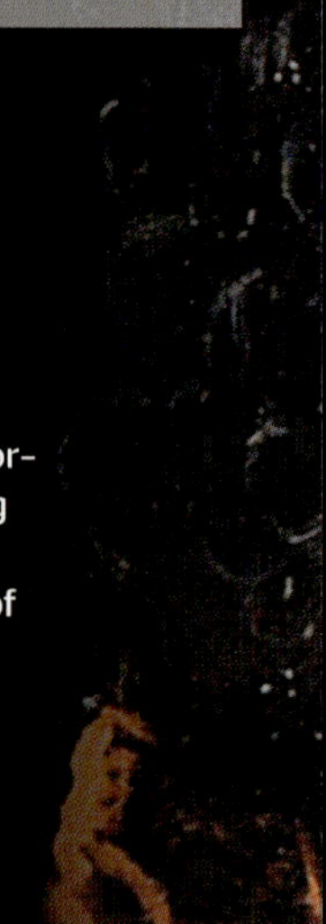

COLD AS ICE
Vlad the Impaler, immortalized in an oil painting from the 16th century preserved in a palace of Innsbruck (Austria).

The Enigma of his Death

Prisoner of the king of Hungary for 12 years, Vlad Draculea recovered the throne of Wallachia in 1476. Everything shows that he dies a short time later in an ambush set by the Turks, victim of treason. Although his body was never found, the legend says he was beheaded and his head sent to Mehmed II.

Was He as Cruel as the Legend Says?

A century after his death, the memory of Vlad Draculea still horrified Europe. He stayed in power a short time, but he used the most extreme violence. It is calculated that he killed more than one hundred thousand people.

The Forest of the Impaled. Engraving that illustrates one of the legends about Vlad's atrocities: his liking of impaling his enemies.

The Case of Jack the Ripper

Between August and November of 1888, a heartless murderer killed and wildly mutilated at least five prostitutes from the Whitchapel neighborhood, in the impoverished zone of East End in London. His identity still unknown, the press made him a legend.

The Five Canonicals

Jack the Ripper's murders exposed the darkest side and the fragile foundations of Victorian society at the end of the 19th century. There are five murders, the Five Canonicals, which were attributed to him without any doubt. According to medical examiner Thomas Bond, the murderer was a male with strong constitution, a great coldness and boldness, who acted by himself. Police could never identify or arrest him.

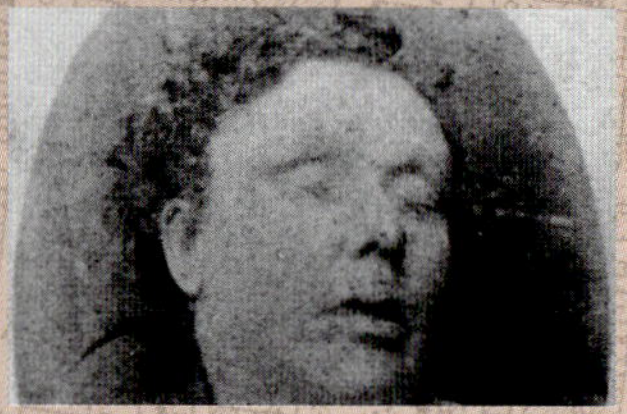

ANNIE CHAPMAN 8-9-1888
Born in 1841, she was separated and had three children.

MARY J. KELLY 9-11-1888
The youngest of the victims was only 25 years old and had been born In Ireland.

CATHERINE EDDOWES 30-9-1888
She was 46 years old and 1.53 m tall. She had been arrested for being drunk and released one hour before her death.

Scenes

1 Buck's Row: 3.40 h
The body was found in front of the gate of some stables, in a dark corner. Having been threatened to be evicted, Nichols had gone out to the street looking for clients.

2 Hanbury Street: 6.20 h
Her body was found in the access to the backyard of a guest house. The homicide had taken place at least two hours earlier.

3 Berner Street: 1.00 h
A jewelry salesman and the employee of a political club found the body. The first one thought that the killer was still around the neighborhood.

4 Mitre Square: 1.45 h
The body with the severed abdomen and mutilated face was found in a dark corner of this plaza with several accesses.

5 Miller's Court, Borset Street: 10.45 h
Murdered in her home, the body of Mary Kelly was discovered by an employee of the landlord.

SENSATIONALISM
The press not only criticized police investigations, it also competed with it, hiring its own detectives.

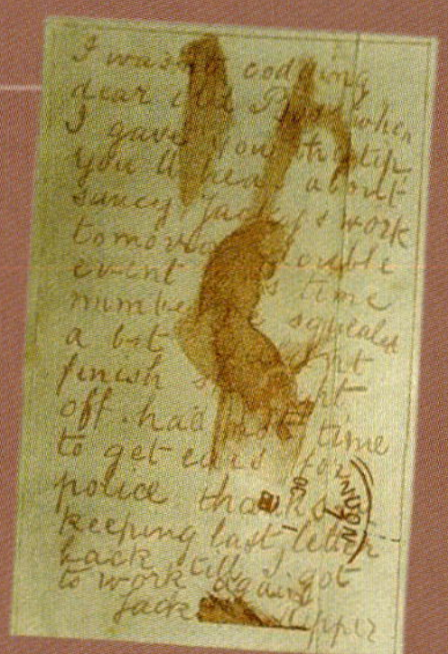

LETTERS
In addition to the dead bodies, the only material evidence of the existence of this killer were some letters and a diary of dubious authorship claimed to belong to Jack the Ripper.

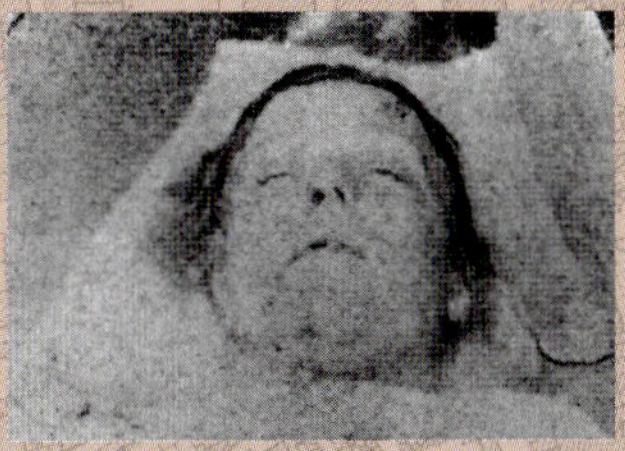

MARY ANN («POLLY») NICHOLS 31-8-1888
Born in 1845, 1.58 m tall. Her alcoholism ruined her marriage, from which she had five children, and it dragged her to make a living on the streets.

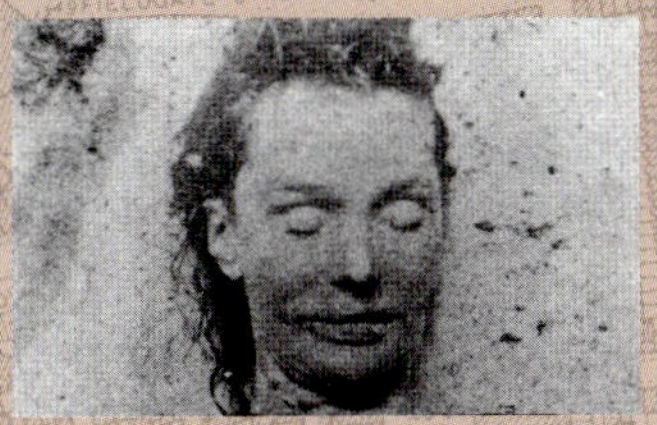

ELIZABETH STRIDE 30-9-1888
She was 44 years old and 1.58 m tall. She had been born in Sweden. She immigrated to London in 1886, where she got married and then separated.

Who Was the Murderer?

The list of suspects was long. The first ones to be signaled were two masters of poisoning of that time: Thomas Neill Cream and George Chapman. Later many more were added, including writer Lewis Carroll, but the real identity of the murderer was never known.

Rasputin and the Romanovs

The enigmatic monk Grigori Rasputin took advantage of the turmoil in which the Russian imperial family was, the Romanovs, in an era of great political and social convulsion, to achieve an enormous influence in the Court of Saint Petersburg.

The Sinister Advisor

In a letter written by Alexandra Feodorovna to her husband Nicholas II, The Russian tsarina stated about Rasputin: "I do not know what would be of us without him. He is our strength and our shelter." How could an illiterate peasant exert so much influence? Alexandra had used healers to cure her son Alexis, sick with hemophilia, and that is how Rasputin arrived to the Court, a well known "santero" (maker of religious Images). This monk, depraved, managed to heal the prince, earning the favor of the tsarina forever. Since then, he exerted total domain over political decision of the pusillanimous tsar Nicholas II.

IN HIS HANDS
Rasputin moves the Tsar and the Tsarina as he wants in this cartoon of a Russian publication of that time.

Who Murdered Rasputin?

Even though Prince Felix Yusupov confessed having killed Grigori Rasputin, there are still many doubts about the author of this murder, since the monk used to have many enemies. There are versions that say that Rasputin was tortured and mutilated; others state that he was offered a gun to commit suicide...

The murderer?
Prince Yusupov, with his wife Irina.

Miracles or Fake?

Visions, accomplished prophecies, incomprehensible healings... Since he was a child, Rasputin, very influenced by orthodox priests and ascetics, was responsible for tens of not very rational deeds. Using that obscurantism he kept on obtaining power. A fake or a chosen one? Today there are still supporters of both opinions.

Tragic End of the Tsars

Three months after Rasputin's death, Tsar Nicholas II was forced to abdicate and the Russian royal family was incarcerated. After 15 months of captivity, it was cruelly murdered in Yekaterinburg. The homicides, led by revolutionary Yaakov Yurovski, hid the bodies and concealed the tombs, feeding this way the last enigma that pursued the Romanovs.

PRISONER
In 1917, Nicholas II, watched over by militaries, prisoner in his residence of Tsarskoye Selo, a short time before his transfer to Tobolsk.

Olga Nicolayevna Romanova
(1895-1918). Eldest daughter of the Tsars.

Tsar Nicholas II
(1868-1918). He succeeded his father, Tsar Alexander III. Cousin of King George V of England.

Tsarina Alexandra Fiodorovna
(1872-1918). Granddaughter of Queen Victoria of England and cousin of Kaiser William II. She married Nicholas II in 1894.

Anna Virubova
(1884-1964). Maid of honor and confidant of the Tsarina. Lover of the Tsar and of Rasputin. She was the one who introduced the monk to the Court, and his nexus with the Tsarina.

Tatiana Nicolayevna Romanova
(1897-1918). Second daughter of the Tsars.

Maria Nicolayevna Romanova
(1899-1918). Third daughter of the Tsars.

Anastasia Nicolayevna Romanova
(1901-1918). For almost one century, there was a legend about her having survived the murder of the Romanovs.

Tsarevich Alexei Romanov
(1904-1918). Youngest son of Nicholas II. His hemophilia was Rasputin's key to enter the palace of the Russian Tsars.

Grigori Rasputin
(1869-1916). His influence upon tsarina Alexandra and other members of the Court gave him protection and a great power.

Aaron Simanovich
(18??-19??). Financial advisor of Rasputin.

Matryona Grigorievna Rasputina
(1898-1977). Second daughter of Rasputin, from his marriage with Praskovia Dubrovina.

Ivan Fiodorovich Manasevich
(18??-19??). Close relative and a kind of secretary of Rasputin. He was a spy with the intelligence service of the Tsar.

Olga Lojtina
(188?-19??). Lady of the Russian high society. Lover and disciple of Rasputin. He taught her how to read and write.

Love Affairs

The assumed infidelities of Tsarina Alexandra, with a constant role in the Russian Court's talk, reached their peak when It was Insinuated that Nicholas II was not the father of Tsarevich Alexei. On the other hand, the Tsar was related with the maid of honor of his wife, Anna Virubova, who was also one of Rasputin's lovers.

Spies of World War II

Espionage accusations in favor of the Nazis reached notable people such as actor Errol Flynn and designer Coco Chanel. Staying out of suspicions, spies played a crucial role in the dispute.

The Other War

War was not only fought in the front. Spying methods developed during the Great War obtained much relevance, both military and political, during World War II. All countries involved spied and were spied. They all created special services that trained thousands of men and women to decipher codes and infiltrate in enemy lines with fake identities. At the end of the war, spying accusations generalized and trivialized, reaching famous people.

Joan Pujol, "Garbo" / "Arabel"

Pujol was a famous Spanish double agent who gave the Nazis false information about the date and place of the allied landing in Normandy. He fooled the German to a point in which Hitler gave him a medal.

Richard Sorge, "Ramsay"

From a German father, Sorge spied for Stalin pretending to be a Nazi news reporter. From Tokyo, he informed Moscow about the date of *Operation Red Beard*, and contributed to the Soviet victory telling distrusting Stalin that Japanese would not attack him.

Mistrust. Prejudices about Sorge prevented Stalin from believing the precise information that he gave him.

Errol Flynn, in the Eyesight

Errol Flynn was accused of spying for the Nazis and Japanese, although there is no real evidence. The rumor started with a picture of the actor appearing in a European magazine, taken in Spain In 1937, with a German soldiers battalion, where they did not specify which side they belonged to. British investigated him too, for having met with Sean Russell, general superintendent of the IRA.

RELATIONSHIP WITH ERBEN
Anti-Semitic and racist, Flynn was investigated by the FBI due to his relationship with Nazi spy Herman Erben, in the image next to the actor.

Errol Flynn. The actor was suspected of trying to turn the Irish to the German side.

MAFIA AND THE ALLIES
When the allies arrived to Sicily, Mafia members were waiting for them with open arms and a well prepared terrain. This alliance was forged several months before in New York between gangster Lucky Luciano (in the image) and the US government .

Operation Modellhut

According to writer Hal Vaughan, Coco Chanel designed *Operation Modellhut* with her lover, general of the SS Walter Schellenberg. It consisted in transmitting to Churchill, through the British embassy in Madrid, a trustable proposal to end the hostilities between the allies and Germany.

SUCCESSFUL DESIGNER
Feminist icon, Coco Chanel was one of the great fashion, perfumes and make-up creators of the 20th century.

Coco Chanel, "Westminster"

The French designer was in the payroll of spies of the Abwehr since 1941 with agent number 7124, and made missions in Madrid and Berlin. In 1944 she was arrested by the Purging Committee of Free France, but released thanks to the intervention of Winston Churchill, who wanted to avoid her to reveal the pro Nazi sympathies of the British high society.

Hitler's Death

The official story claims that the *fuehrer* committed suicide in his bunker, but other versions claim that he was murdered or, as Soviet leader Stalin claimed, he had managed to escape from Germany and hidden in a safe place.

In the Bunker

According to his personal diary, Hitler spent his last months in the bunker of the chancellery until, one week before the definite surrender of Nazi Germany, on May 8th, 1945, he decided to commit suicide. Even though there are versions that claim he was murdered by his personal guard, or even that he managed to escape, his closest collaborators claimed that he took his life with a shot to avoid an end like Mussolini's in Italy.

GENERATORS
The constant buzzing of the electric generators and water pumps of the bunker made it hard to hear a detonation.

SECURITY
All the doors of the bunker were airtight, anticipating a gas attack.

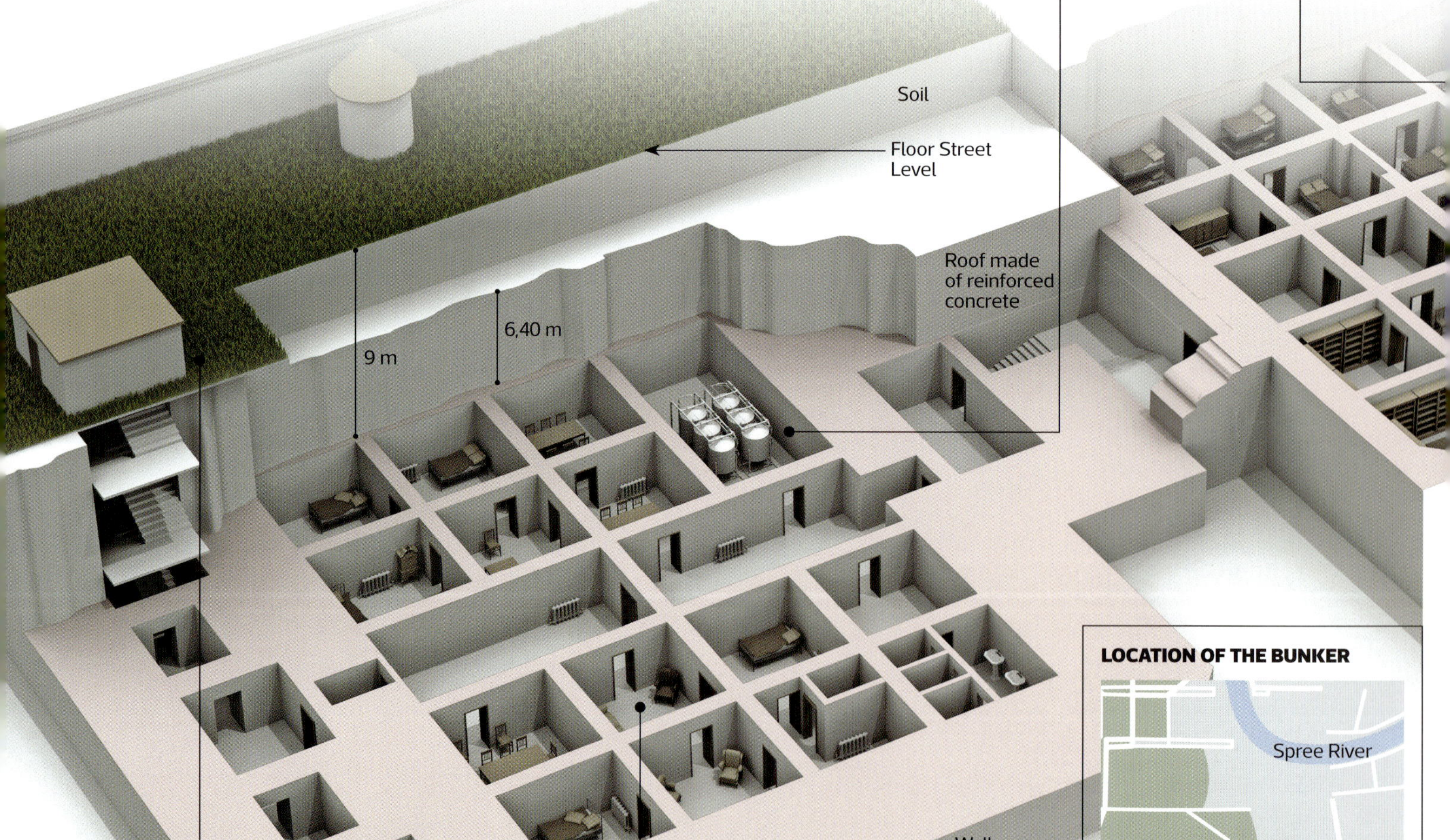

CREMATION
The bodies of Adolf Hitler and Eva Braun would have been cremated a few meters away from the exit to the garden.

CABINET
The lifeless bodies of the *fuehrer* and his wife would have been found on the sofa of this living room.

LOCATION OF THE BUNKER

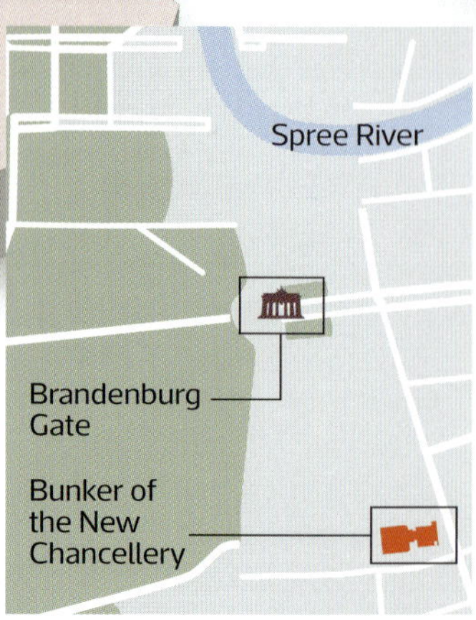

Soviet Occultism

Inside the bunker, they found blood on the sofa where supposedly Hitler had committed suicide. This and other evidences remained in Stalin's hands, who hid everything he knew from everybody. The Kremlin has acknowledged officially that in 1970 the remains of the dictator were destroyed, buried secretly in Magdeburg since 1946.

FRAGMENT OF A SKULL They picked it up from the crater where they discovered Hitler's remains, but it has been dismissed that it belonged to him.

Did He Escape Alive?

There Is also the hypotheses that Hitler would have been able to escape to Norway, where a submarine would have taken him to Argentina, staying there to live with Eva Braun and his two sons until his death in 1962. The truth is that In 1945 there were many German submarine sightings in front of the coasts of Argentina. Two of them, the U-530 and the U-977, were especially investigated.

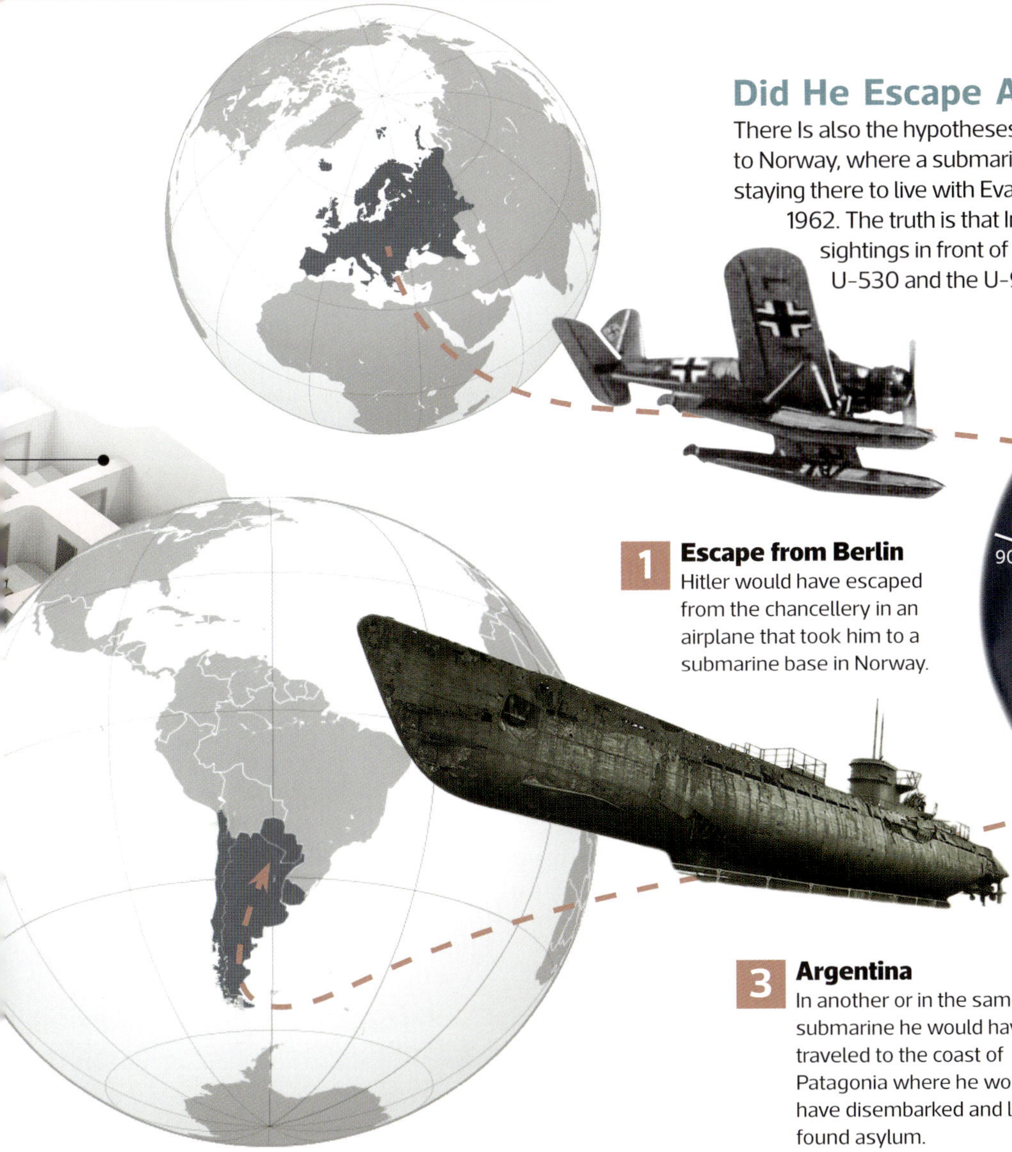

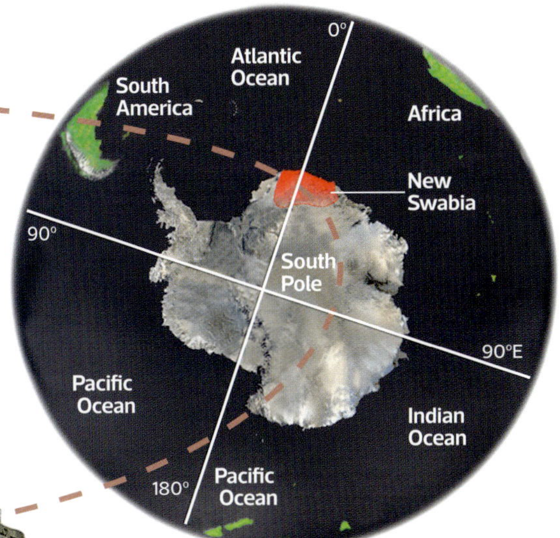

1 Escape from Berlin Hitler would have escaped from the chancellery in an airplane that took him to a submarine base in Norway.

2 Antarctic Base On board a submarine he would have sailed to a base of New Swabia, the zone of Antarctica explored by the Nazis before the war.

3 Argentina In another or in the same submarine he would have traveled to the coast of Patagonia where he would have disembarked and later found asylum.

The Fuehrer's Tomb

On May 4th, after an intense search, soviet agents would have found two cremated bodies buried in a crater of the garden at the Chancellery of the Reich, supposedly Hitler and Eva Braun's. Harry Mengershausen, a guard of the bunker was witness of the cremation, sometime later he confirmed that this was the exact place where the couple had been cremated and buried. In the image on the right, the crater of the garden that kept the cremated bodies.

Secret Operations of the CIA

Experimenting with drugs to control the mind, training killers with hypnosis or the development of chemical and biological agents are part of the sinister story of the Central Intelligence Agency (CIA) during the Cold War.

The "Family Jewels"

The CIA, American espionage agency founded In 1947, carried out some pretty surprising projects and practices out of the law in the past. We have learned about many of them thanks to declassification of a series of documents known as the "Family Jewels." The colored dots in the map show the places where they experimented, plotted or executed these secret projects and operations.

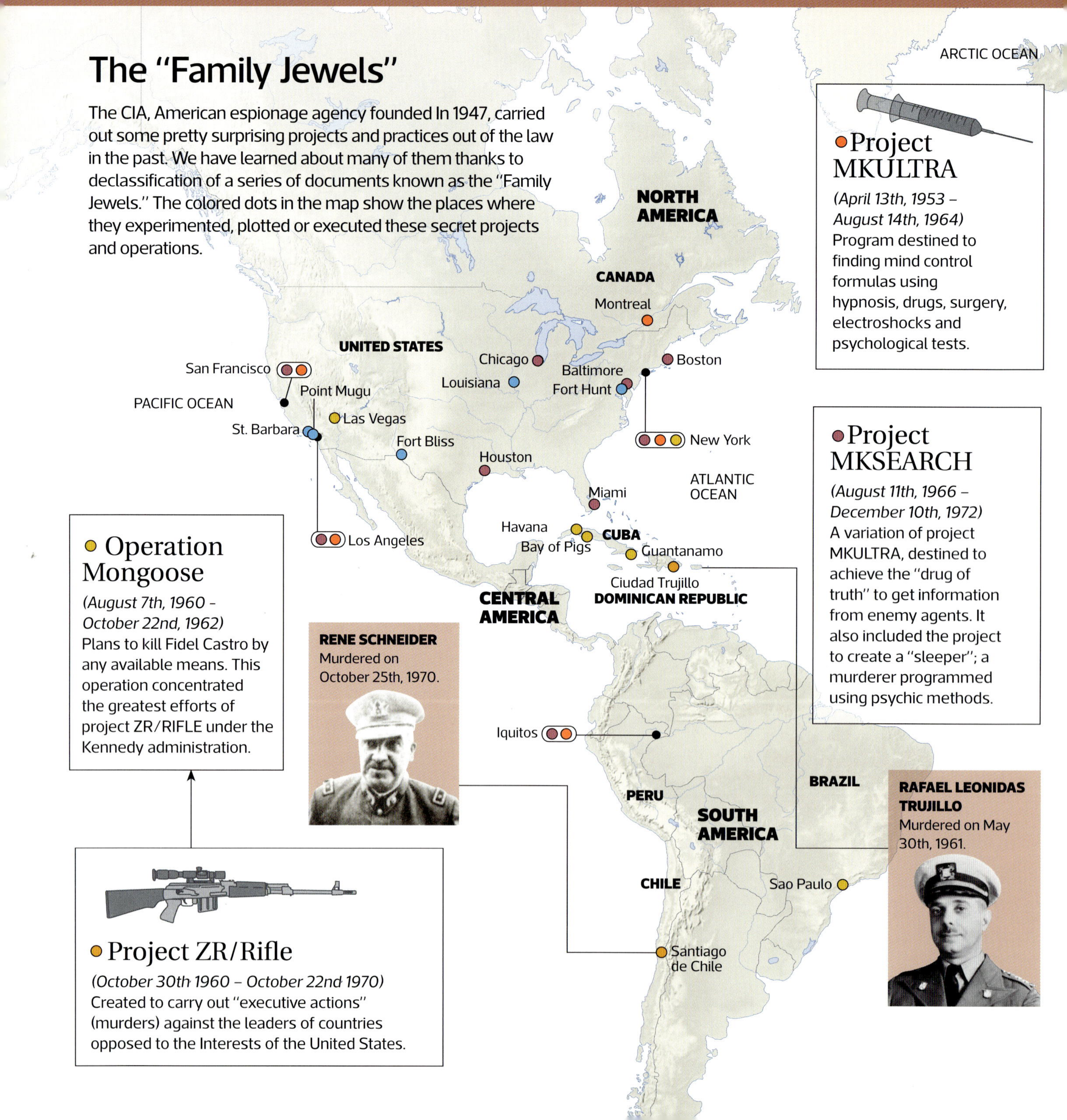

Project MKULTRA

(April 13th, 1953 – August 14th, 1964)
Program destined to finding mind control formulas using hypnosis, drugs, surgery, electroshocks and psychological tests.

Project MKSEARCH

(August 11th, 1966 – December 10th, 1972)
A variation of project MKULTRA, destined to achieve the "drug of truth" to get information from enemy agents. It also included the project to create a "sleeper"; a murderer programmed using psychic methods.

Operation Mongoose

(August 7th, 1960 - October 22nd, 1962)
Plans to kill Fidel Castro by any available means. This operation concentrated the greatest efforts of project ZR/RIFLE under the Kennedy administration.

RENE SCHNEIDER
Murdered on October 25th, 1970.

RAFAEL LEONIDAS TRUJILLO
Murdered on May 30th, 1961.

Project ZR/Rifle

(October 30th 1960 – October 22nd 1970)
Created to carry out "executive actions" (murders) against the leaders of countries opposed to the Interests of the United States.

Agent in a Hypnotic Trance?

Sirhan Sirhan's lawyer, the man who shot Robert Kennedy, claimed that his defendant had been "programmed" against his will to murder the senator. Public opinion also believed that the younger brother of the murdered president John F. Kennedy had been a victim of a conspiracy.

Murder. On the left, Robert Kennedy just after he had been shot. On the right, Palestinian Sirhan Sirhan.

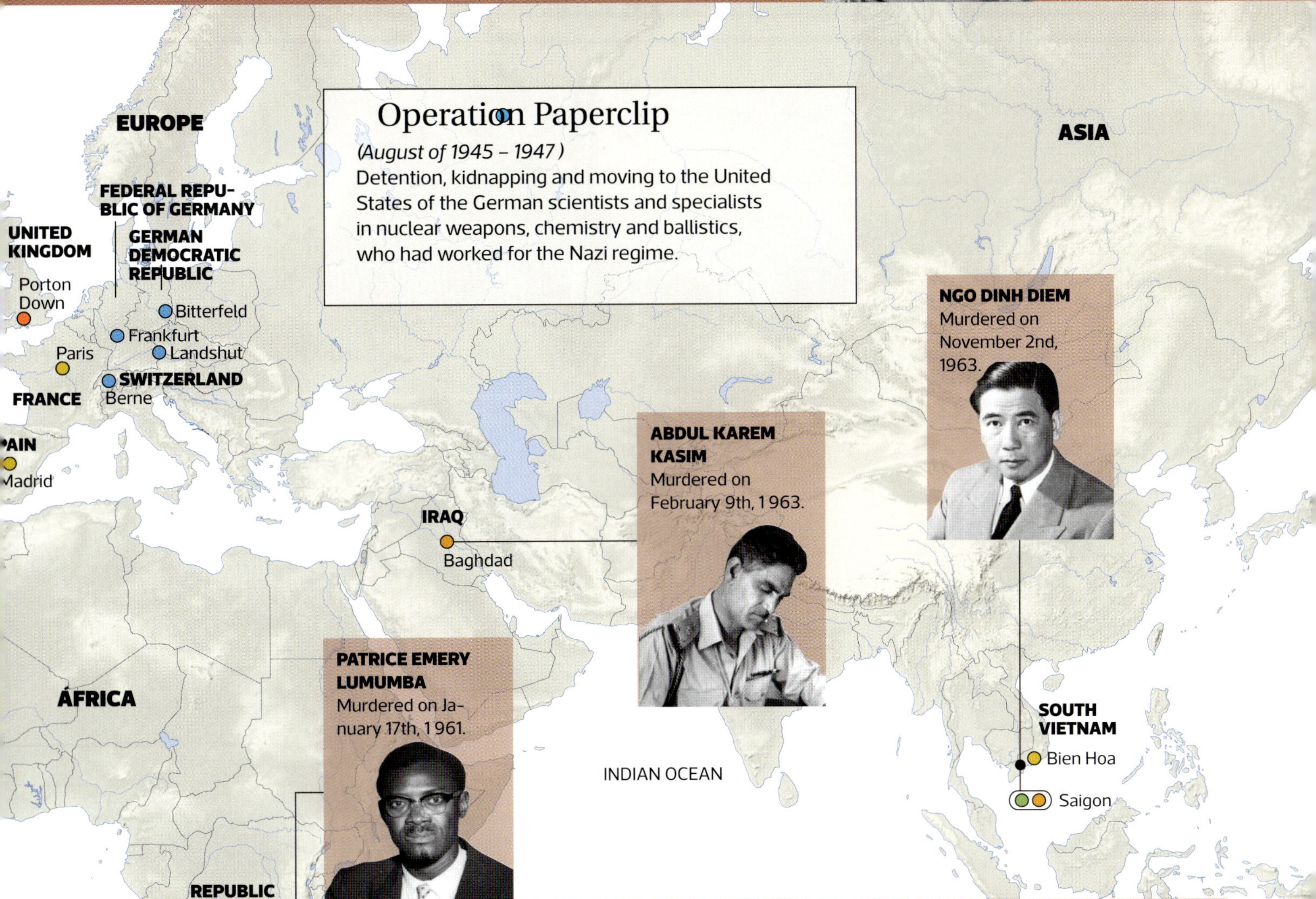

Operation Paperclip

(August of 1945 – 1947)
Detention, kidnapping and moving to the United States of the German scientists and specialists in nuclear weapons, chemistry and ballistics, who had worked for the Nazi regime.

NGO DINH DIEM
Murdered on November 2nd, 1963.

ABDUL KAREM KASIM
Murdered on February 9th, 1963.

PATRICE EMERY LUMUMBA
Murdered on January 17th, 1961.

Project Phoenix

(January of 1968 –August of 1971)
Program for detention and elimination of supports of Vietcong guerrilla. It caused thousands of civilian victims in South Vietnam.

Mafia Help

The CIA conceived hundreds of plans to kill Castro: bomb or poisoned cigars, explosive mollusks... For this, it counted with collaboration of the biggest capos of the Mafia, among them Sam Giancana and John Roselli.

Obsession. The Kennedy brothers put pressure on the CIA to eliminate the Cuban leader anyway they could.

Return from Death

Those who have had the so called Near-Death Experiences (NDE) claim that they have abandoned their bodies, seen luminous beings, felt a supernatural world. They all agree in that what they lived changed their lives forever.

What is an NDE?

Since man exists on earth, knowing what happens after death has been one of its great obsessions. The closest to this is the testimony of the people that have lived a Near-Death Experience, that is, the impressions or memories of people that have overcome a clinical death or that have been close to dying. Only one out of three people that go through this experience dare to tell about it and the testimonies are always very similar.

Differences

Not all elements of which there is evidence in the NDE are always present in all of them. It is considered that, of the 10 steps that summarize them, at least four must be present in order to be considered a Near-Death Experience. There are no two identical stories, and the order of the phases is not always the same.

The Ten Steps of a NDE

1 Trauma
The patient experiments the NDE after an accident or the failure of one or several organs. If possible, the doctor initiates the reanimation process.

2 Liberation
During the NDE many people claim having experimented a felling of liberation, of absence of any kind of pain and/or worry.

3 Release
Abandoning of the physical body. Some people get to see their body from outside and experiment a sharpening of the senses.

4 Tunnel
One of the most generalized experiences in NDE is, after listening to a loud noise, appearing suddenly in a tunnel.

5 Light
Another constant is the presence of a very bright light that dominates everything that surrounds the person, accompanied with a feeling of peace.

Why There Are No Historical Examples

Many people who "came back from death" would have not been able to do it in other times due to the lack of technical methods (defibrillators, adrenaline injections in the heart and other innovations). This could be the reason why these historical cases are not known, although the topic has not been studied deeply.

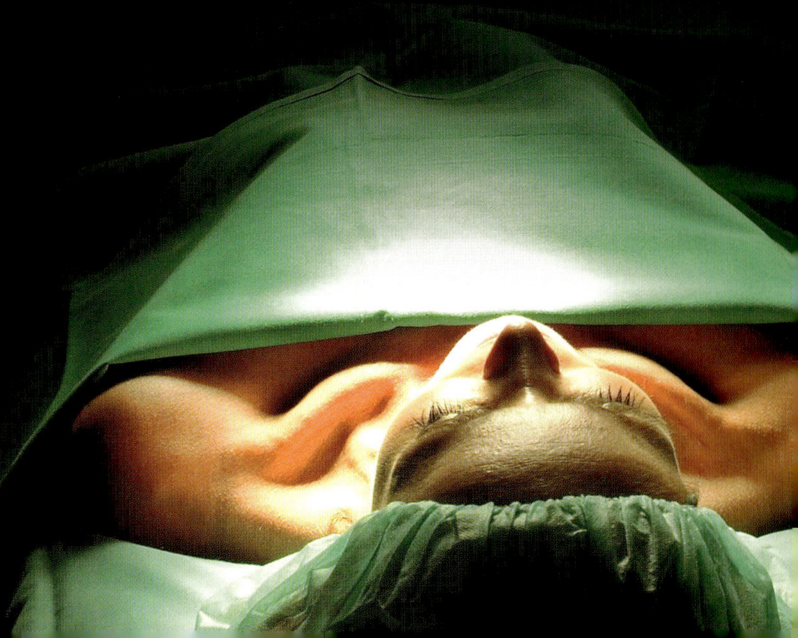

The Precursor

Philosopher and psychologist Raymond A. Moody was the first one to describe the NDE episodes from a testimony from 150 people. Considered a world expert on the topic, his work has had an enormous impact, although it has not achieved the unanimous support of the scientific community.

What Science Says

Science has been trying to give an explanation to NDE for years. For instance, it has been proved that some anesthetic drugs have a "dissociative" effect, that is, they can make the receptor feel "separated" from his own body and that, also, he experiments hallucinations and "very real" dreams.

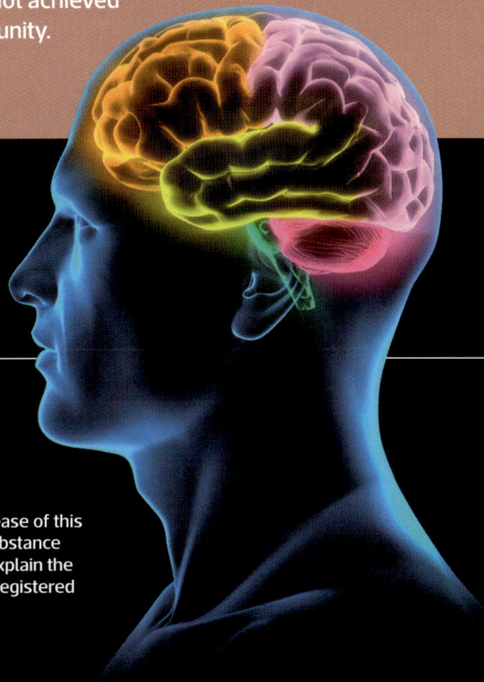

Serotonin. The increase of this neurotransmitter substance in the brain would explain the feeling of pleasure registered in many cases.

6 Revision
Some people point out that they had done a panoramic review of their lives; others claim having had flashes about events still to happen.

7 Reunion
The feeling of infinite love is often related with the presence of already dead loved ones. They are known as "beings of light."

8 Decision
The "beings of light" seem to be, in many cases, the ones in charge of announcing that the moment to cross the threshold to the beyond has not arrived.

9 Return
After the decision, many times accom-panied by a refusal to return, a feeling of arriving to a frontier is experimented: the "return" to the body.

10 Afterwards
It is calculated that only one out of three people that overcome clinical death keeps conscience of the NDE. From them, only a few dare to tell about what happened.

The Miracles of Lourdes

When all hope has been lost, there is only the miracle left. Each year, around six millions of believers go to the Sanctuary of Our Lady of Lourdes in search of scientifically unexplained cures, which they attribute to divine intervention.

The Apparition of the Virgin

Between February 11th and July 16th of 1858, Virgin Mary appeared 18 times In front of the girl Bernadette Soubirous in a grotto near Lourdes, a small locality of the French Pyrenees. On March 25th the Virgin gave her name: "I am the immaculate Conception." The authenticity of the apparitions was recognized in 1862 by the Catholic Church. Since then, millions of people visit the Sanctuary of Our Lady of Lourdes to be healed by its miraculous water.

THE MIRACULOUS NUMBERS

▸ **Apparitions:**	18
▸ **Official miraculous healings:**	67
▸ **Inexplicable healings:**	7.000

THE TEMPLE
The Virgin asked Bernadette to have a chapel built there. The Basilica of the Immaculate Conception was raised over the grotto In 1872 by Monsignor Laurence.

BASILICA OF OUR LADY OF THE ROSARY
It was built between 1883 and 1889. In the front esplanade the famous blessing of the sick takes place.

Premature Death

Some years after the apparition of the Virgin, young Bernadette Soubirous (1844-1879) left her life as a shepherdess to begin the novitiate at Nevers convent. However, a short time later with only 35 years of age, she died due to bone tuberculosis. She was canonized in 1933.

MIRACULOUS WATER?
The analyzes show that the water of Lourdes is not special, and Bernadette herself regretted that it was seen as medicine. Despite that, pilgrims keep their unalterable faith in the power of the water.

THE ROCK
Pilgrims touch the rock of the cave where the Virgin appeared trying to get Its energy.

THE GROTTO AND THE STATUE
The grotto, formed by three cavities, the mass taking place in the largest one, keeps the image of the Virgin, located in a niche two meters high, right in the place where it is said that the Virgin used to appear to Bernadette Soubirous.

SPRING
The Virgin ordered Bernadette to wash her hands and drink the water of the grotto, which immediately acquired the fame of being miraculous.

THE SANCTUARY

- Place of the apparitions
- Basilica
- Chapel
- Reception center for the sick

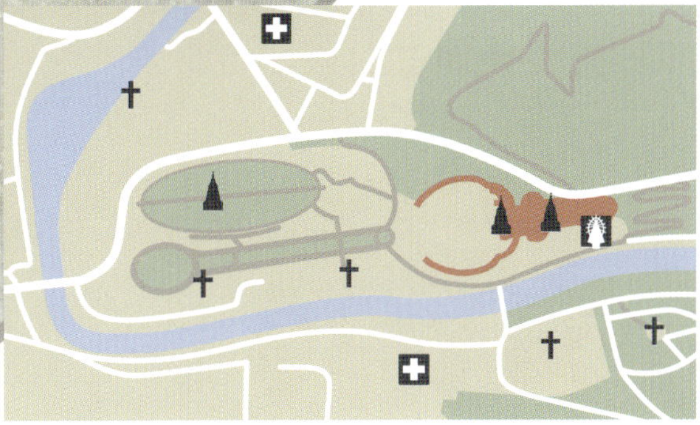

Chapter 3

Lost Civilizations

Did cities like Atlantis or Troy really exist? What was the real reason of the collapse of the Maya Civilization in Middle America, or the Minoan in Crete and the Rapa Nui in Easter Island?

If Xia dynasty (2070-1600 BC) of China, considered as legendary by historians for many centuries, became real due to the discovery of graves and objects on a date as recent as 1959, we cannot discard that some legends can have, at least a little bit of reality. Troy itself is an example of that. The legend of the war between Greek and Trojans arrived to us only through the Homeric poems, which made later historians doubt about this event and even about the existence of the city. But currently, most archeologists assure that the remains correspond with part of the site dug by Heinrich Schliemann in Turkey at the end of the 19th century.

Nothing has been discovered about Atlantis, which has been searched for unsuccessfully in the Mediterranean Sea and the Atlantic Ocean by many researchers, nor about the mythical city of El Dorado, although some evidences have arisen showing that in the Amazonia there was a civilization unknown until now, which could have built the golden metropolis. Hypotheses and guesses will last the time these legends live on.

Atlantis

This famous lost city is one of the biggest enigmas of history, since it is not known with certainty if it really existed. The firs mention of Atlantis goes back to the 5th century BC: philosopher Plato refers to it in his famous Dialogues.

Real or Invented?

Greek thinker Plato dedicated part of his dialogues *Timaeus and Critias* to talk about Atlantis, giving it detailed descriptions. For some historians there Is no doubt about the historical existence of that civilization, while for others it is just fiction created by Plato as a critique to maritime expansionism of Athens. According to the Platonic text, the city was formed by a central island, where the Acropolis was located, surrounded by concentric rings of land separated by water channels.

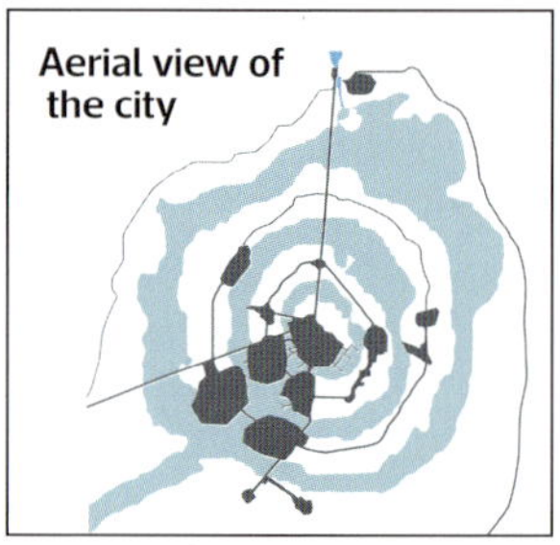

Who Ruled Atlantis?

According to Plato, the island was ruled by ten kings (in its origin, five pairs of twins), who got together every five years and judged all those who had broken the laws, affixed on an orichalcum column in front of the temple of Poseidon. The first twin (maximum king) had the name of Atlas.

ATLAS
Mythology says that Atlas, name from which the name of the island and the surrounding sea came from, was condemned by Zeus to carry the pillars of the Earth.

Ruins of Akrotiri

The diggings made in the island of Thera, current Santorini, allowed the reconstruction of an ancient society maybe related with Atlantis. Under a layer of volcanic remains, there were houses and numerous amphorae. Also beautiful frescos with images of daily life.

Conservation. The volcanic mantle preserved the site of Akrotiri, which is dated In the 2nd millennium BC.

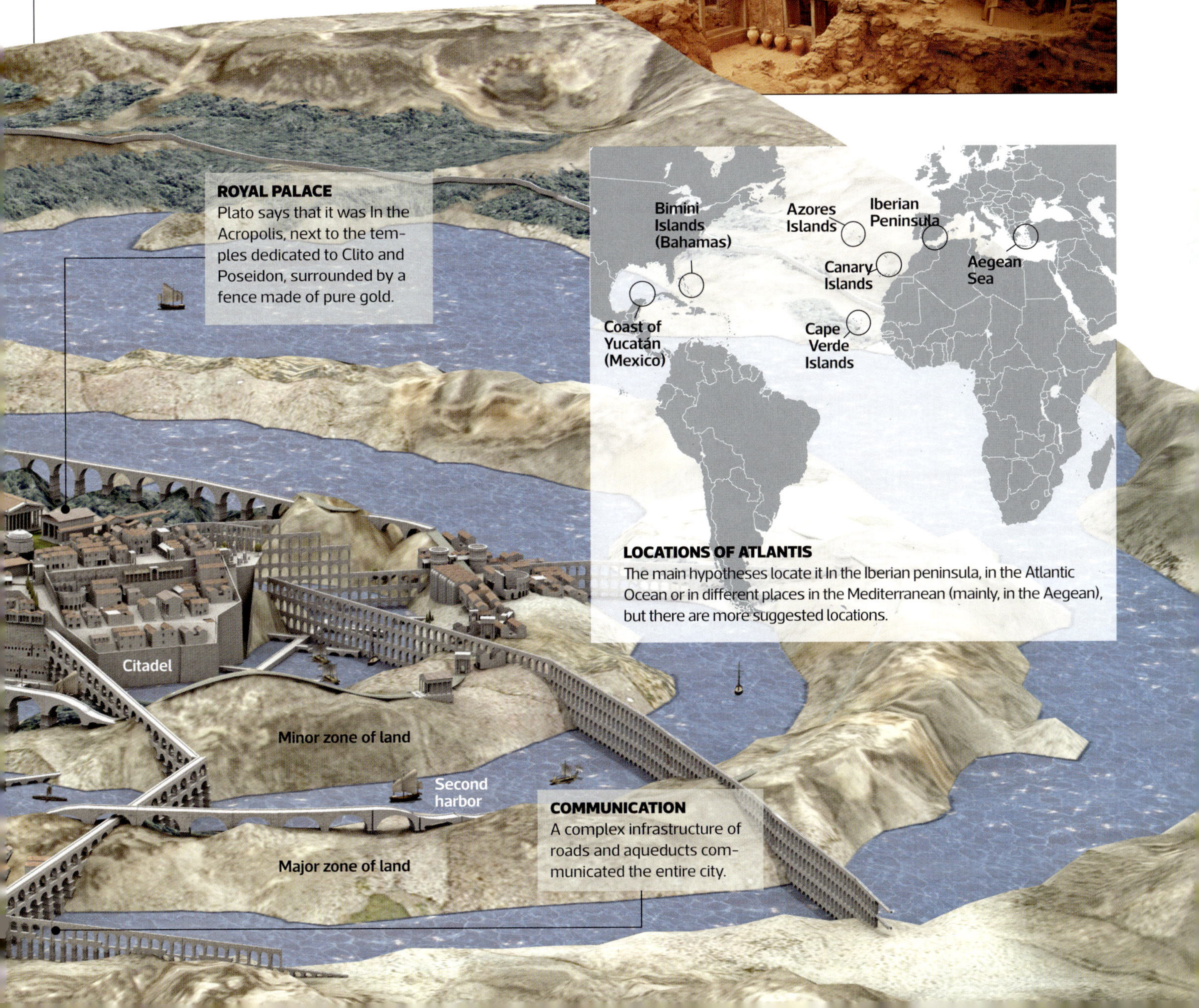

ROYAL PALACE
Plato says that it was In the Acropolis, next to the temples dedicated to Clito and Poseidon, surrounded by a fence made of pure gold.

COMMUNICATION
A complex infrastructure of roads and aqueducts communicated the entire city.

LOCATIONS OF ATLANTIS
The main hypotheses locate it In the Iberian peninsula, in the Atlantic Ocean or in different places in the Mediterranean (mainly, in the Aegean), but there are more suggested locations.

Dholavira, the City of Water

The Indus Valley civilization, which developed by horse between the 3rd and 2nd millennium BC in the region located between the current Pakistan and India, built great engineering works In cities such as Dholavira, and hides several enigmas for the scholars.

Masters of Urbanism

Dholavira, farming and commercial city of the Indus had an advanced urban planning. Besides residential neighborhoods formed by straight streets and well distributed houses, it had sewer and water collection systems. Its inhabitants knew how to adapt well to the rise of rivers during the monsoon season.

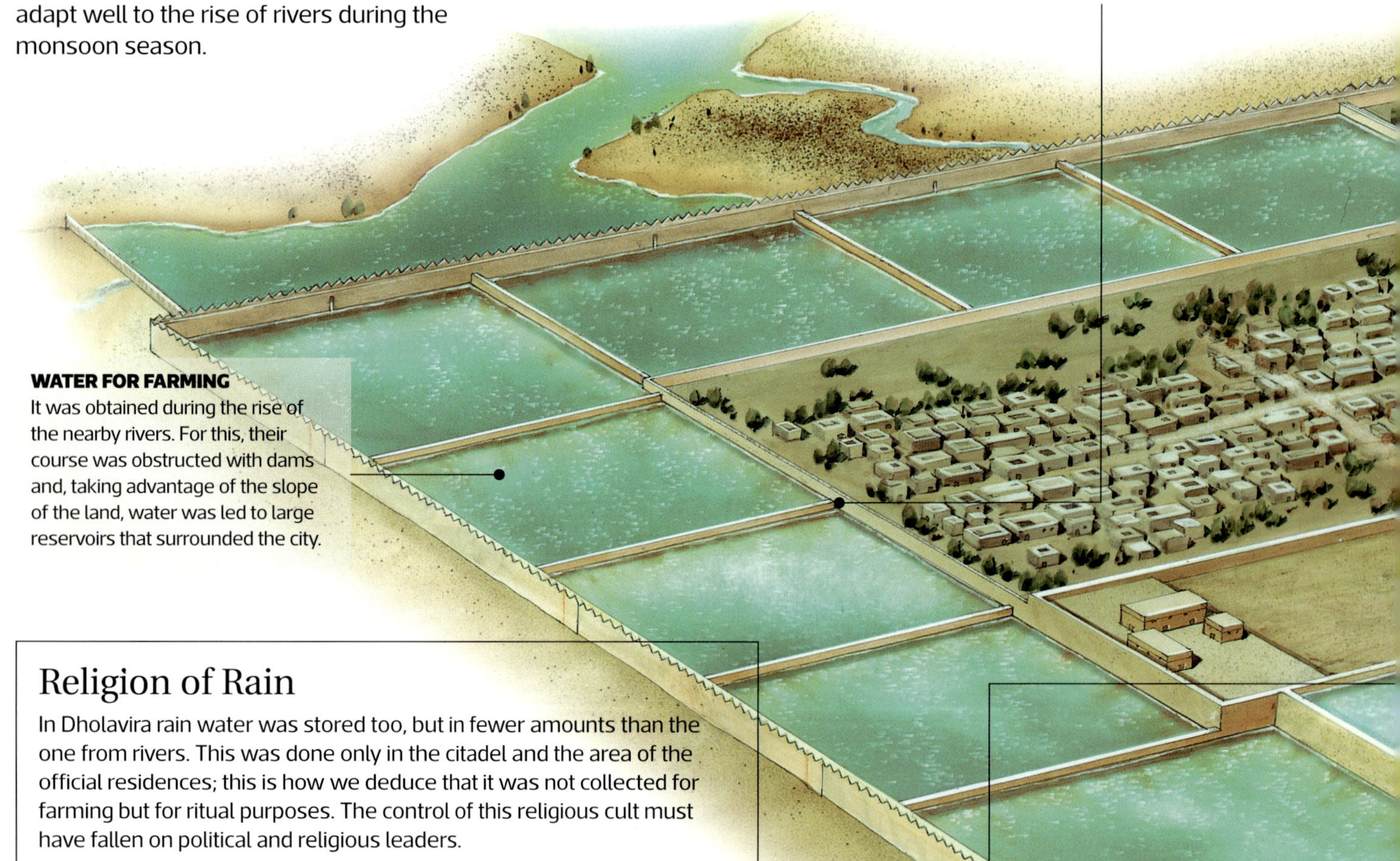

SEWAGE SYSTEM
Placed around big avenues, the houses of the residential towns incorporated sewage systems connected with a network of underground sewers.

WATER FOR FARMING
It was obtained during the rise of the nearby rivers. For this, their course was obstructed with dams and, taking advantage of the slope of the land, water was led to large reservoirs that surrounded the city.

OFFICIAL RESIDENCES
The houses of the ruling or more favored sectors of the city were located in this special precinct, to which one could access only from the citadel.

Religion of Rain

In Dholavira rain water was stored too, but in fewer amounts than the one from rivers. This was done only in the citadel and the area of the official residences; this is how we deduce that it was not collected for farming but for ritual purposes. The control of this religious cult must have fallen on political and religious leaders.

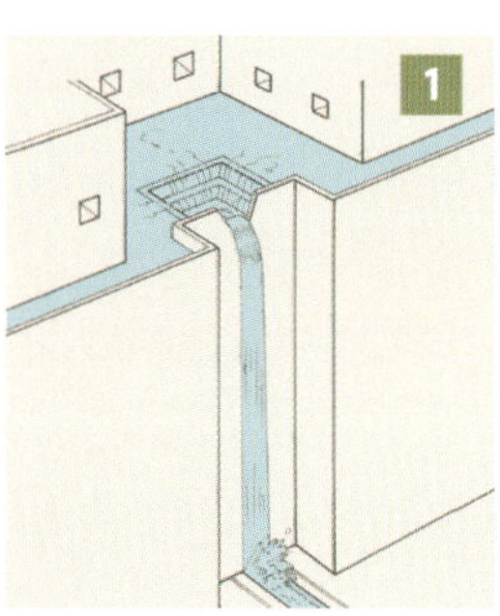

1.Collector. Located in the highest part of the wall, it took the water to the pond of the official residences through a canal.

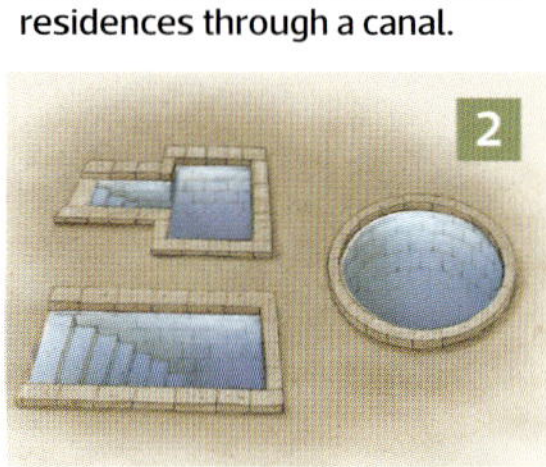

2. Well and baths. Located in open air and in the southern sector of the citadel, it was probably used to make ritual ablutions.

Who Ruled over the Indus Cities?

Only few remains of weapons and traces of armies have been found in the ruins of the cities of the Indus civilization. This could be due to the fact that they were ruled by ascetics who subjugated the people by means of spirituality. Another hypothesis is that there may have been representations of battles or military commanders in perishable materials that were not preserved.

Spear Heads. These copper pieces found in the Indus Valley are preserved in the National Museum of New Delhi.

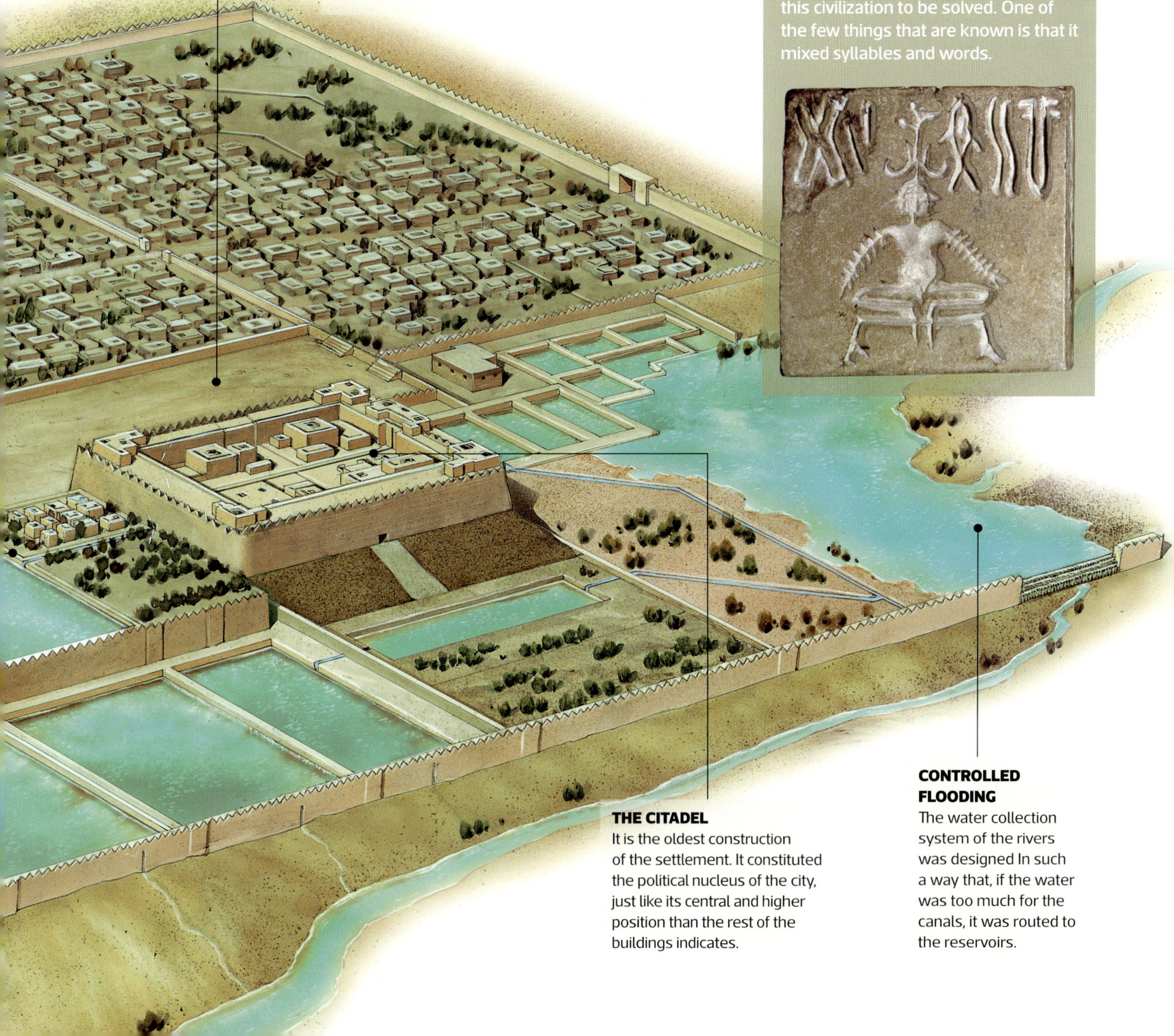

CEREMONIAL PATIO
The great esplanade that separated the citadel from the towns was the place for the celebration of public events. Over the lintel of the door of the citadel there was a great board with ten symbols that have not been deciphered.

THE CITADEL
It is the oldest construction of the settlement. It constituted the political nucleus of the city, just like its central and higher position than the rest of the buildings indicates.

CONTROLLED FLOODING
The water collection system of the rivers was designed In such a way that, if the water was too much for the canals, it was routed to the reservoirs.

Mysterious Writing

To this date, the writing system of the Indus has been undecipherable, which has prevented many enigmas about this civilization to be solved. One of the few things that are known is that it mixed syllables and words.

Minoan Civilization

Between 2700 and 1450 BC, in the island of Crete in the Aegean Sea, a powerful and brilliant civilization appeared, on which there are still many questions. Minoans left a writing system that has not been deciphered, an exquisite art and the legend of the Minotaur.

The Great Palace of Knossos

Minoan civilization owes its name to its discoverer, archeologist Sir Arthur Evans, who related (probably mistakenly) the Cretan palace of Knossos with the residence of legendary King Minos and the myth of the Minotaur. This huge building, with more than a thousand rooms distributed in two hectares, was the referent of the Minoan culture, just like other similar palaces that served as epicenter of an economic activity based mainly on maritime trade.

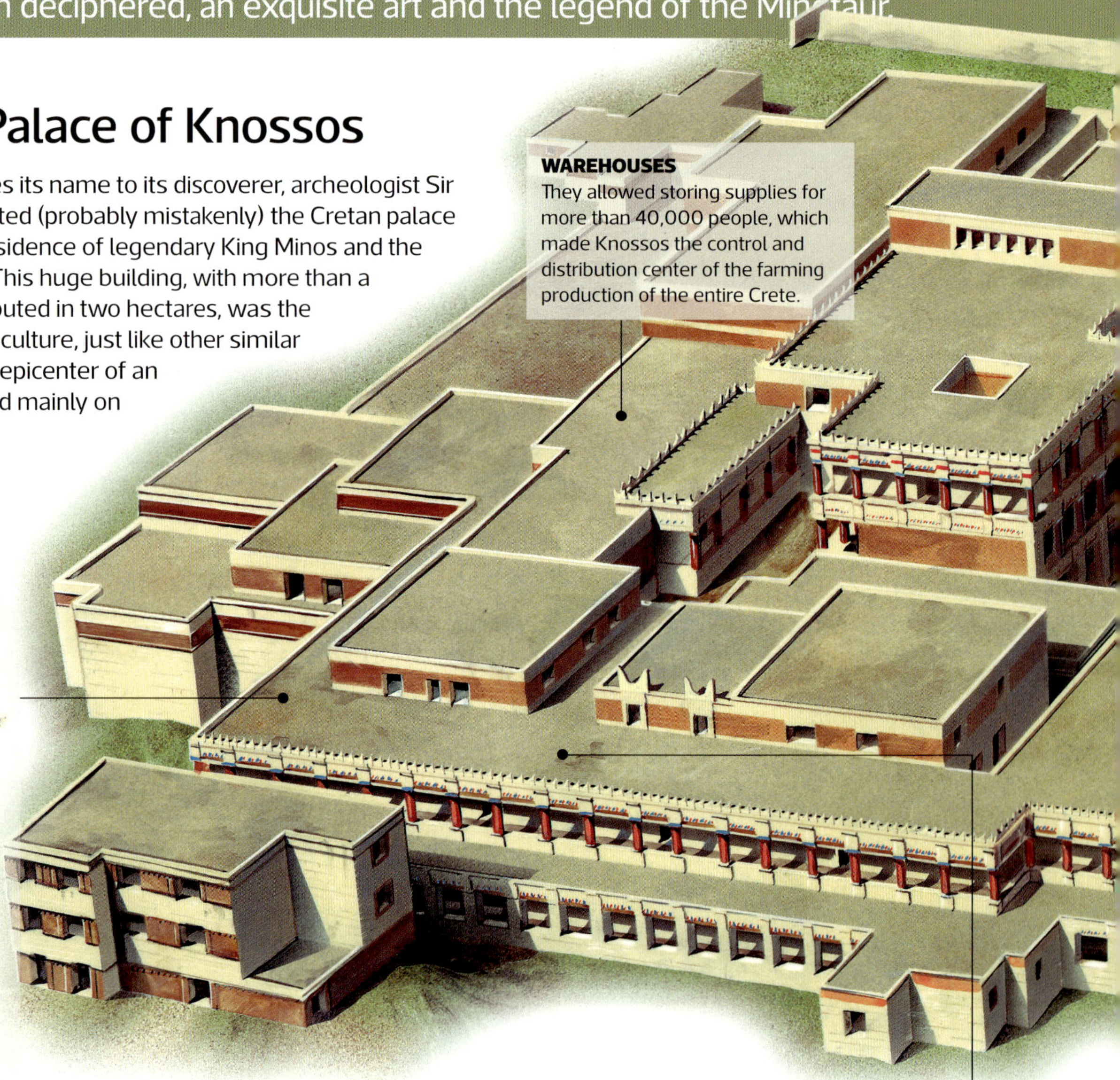

WAREHOUSES
They allowed storing supplies for more than 40,000 people, which made Knossos the control and distribution center of the farming production of the entire Crete.

THE PRINCE OF LIS
This character is included in a mural painting of the hall that communicates the southern gate with the religious rooms.

SOUTHERN GATE
It communicated the southeast entrance with the central patio. Just like the rest of the halls in the precinct, it was placed on wooden columns with the shape of an Inverted cone.

Minoan Chronology

6000 BC	2700 BC	2000 BC	1700 BC	1450 BC	1400 BC
Neolithic culture Dispersed settlements and predominance of agriculture as a way of subsistence.	**Pre palace period** Also called Ancient Minoan, it is a stage of formation of the Minoan culture.	**Ancient Palaces** Development of trade and great palaces, which succumbed to an earthquake.	**Modern Palaces** After the reconstruction of the palaces, a new boom and expansion of Minoan culture.	**Eruption** Thera Volcano (Santorini) destroys the palaces one more time and Minoan decline begins.	**Post palaces period** A decline stage is produced, which ended with Mycenaean domination.

The Legend of the Minotaur

According to Greek mythology, the Minotaur was a monster with the head of a bull and the body of a man, born from the union of Pasiphae (wife of King Minos of Crete) and a bull sent by Poseidon. The Minotaur was locked in the underground labyrinths of Knossos until Theseus killed it.

THE JUMPING OF THE BULL
This game is represented in the Minoan frescos. Young people held on to the horns of the animal to jump over its back.

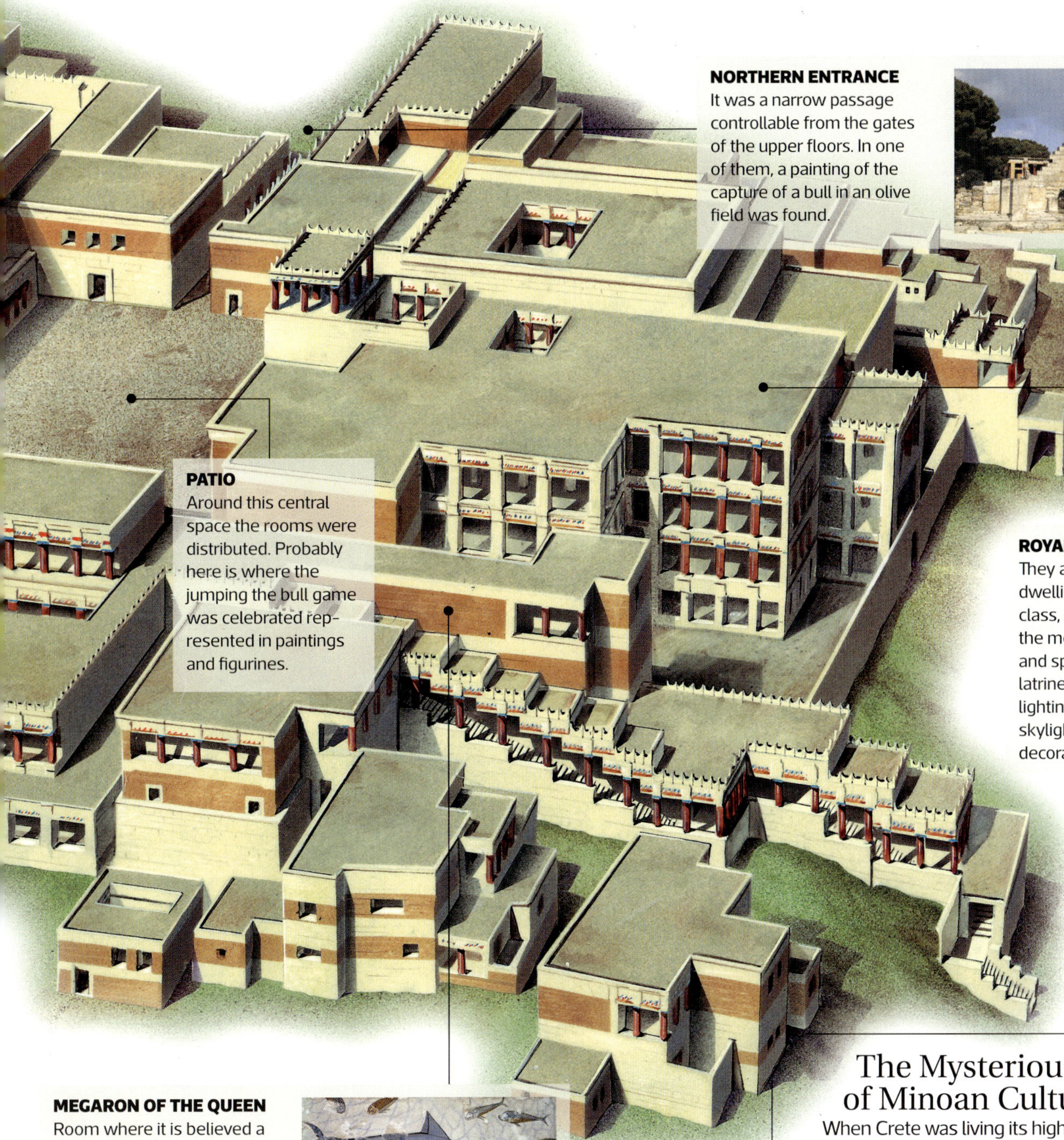

NORTHERN ENTRANCE
It was a narrow passage controllable from the gates of the upper floors. In one of them, a painting of the capture of a bull in an olive field was found.

PATIO
Around this central space the rooms were distributed. Probably here is where the jumping the bull game was celebrated represented in paintings and figurines.

ROYAL CHAMBERS
They are considered the dwellings of the ruling class, since they were the most complete and spacious. They had latrines In each room, lighting system using skylights and abundant decoration.

MEGARON OF THE QUEEN
Room where it is believed a royal ruler lived. It has one of the spectacular mural frescos with a naturalistic scene that decorated the inside of the palace.

The Mysterious End of Minoan Culture

When Crete was living its highest splendor, it is believed that the eruption of Thera volcano, in the current island of Santorini, caused huge waves, earthquakes and ash rain that would have destroyed the palaces and made people go away. Mycenaean people took advantage of the situation to occupy the island.

The Trojan War

Axis of the Greek-Latin epic, the Trojan War, whose existence is still questioned, was narrated in a cycle of poems by Homer, of which only two have reached these days intact: the *Iliad* and the *Odyssey.*

Homer's Word

Despite being one of the most notable events of Ancient times, the Trojan War raises doubts among modern erudite. The most famous text that narrates this conflict, Homer's *Iliad*, is an epic poem and not a history book, and has a lot of supernatural events. In addition, it was written centuries after the events it describes, dated around 1200 BC, while the *Iliad* dates approximately from the year 700 BC.

What Caused the War?

The Homeric legend says that Paris, prince of Troy, kidnapped Helen (in the image) at her husband Melenaus' house, in Sparta, and took her to his kingdom, unleashing the war between Greeks and Trojans. Helen's beauty, however, was able to hide really a commercial conflict, since Troy occupied a strategic and coveted location.

HOMER, 8TH CENTURY BC
His epic poems narrate the Trojan War, the abduction of Helen by Paris, and the deeds of Hector and Achilles.

THE POWER OF MYCENAE
Mycenae gathered the Greek armies to direct them to Asia Minor with the objective of destroying Troy. According to Homer, the Greek forces added up to 1,184 ships and 70,000 men. However, more recent calculations talk about 300 ships and 15,000 men.

Did the Trojan Horse Exist?

According to the *Odyssey* and the *Aeneid*, several Greek soldiers hid inside a wooden horse, which the Trojans took for a gift and introduced inside their walls. During the night, they came out and opened the gates of Troy to their army. Some people interpret that the horse was really a war machine; others, that it was a metaphor of the new Greek fleet.

Epeius. Homer narrates that the Greek soldier Epeius (in the image) was ho built the wooden horse.

Chronology

The siege of the Greek armies on Troy lasted ten years, until the city was finally conquered. The war happened during a period of changes in the Aegean Sea and the peak of Mycenae.

2500 BC

Historical Troy

First steps of historical Troy. The city enjoys a strategic position in the Black Sea. It had to be rebuilt many times due to natural catastrophes and occupations.

1450 BC

Splendor of Mycenae

A volcanic eruption in the island of Thera produces a tidal wave that ends with the Cretan fleet. The sudden fall of the Minoan culture leads to the peak of Mycenae and its control in the Aegean Sea.

1250 BC

Trojan War

According to Herodotus, the city of Troy is besieged by Mycenae on that date. Around the year 1,200 BC the end of the Mycenaean kingdoms begins and the migrations of the Ionic and Aeolian towards the Cyclades and the coasts of Asia Minor begin.

The Great Chavin Sanctuary

Beginning in 1,000 BC, the enigmatic ceremonial complex of Chavin de Huantar, on the eastern slope of the Andes, became the great religious epicenter of the region, where pilgrims from all people of the coast, mountains and tropical forest went.

What Did the Figures Symbolize?

The amazing stone carvings found at the site of Chavin de Huantar (Peru), with images of birds, hawks and eagles, felines, jaguars, lizards and snakes with a fierce aspect and human attributes, represented the deities of this culture. The most important carving is the Lanzon, a huge monolith that shows an anthropomorphous being with feline and snake traits. It is believed that with this figures they were trying to intimidate and impress the pilgrims that came here to do their offerings.

MALE DRAGON
This face of the obelisk has the male version of the dragon, which according to archeologist Julio C. Tello is associated with the sky and the rain.

THE FACE
It is the most remarkable element of the obelisk. The enormous teeth with the shape of disks of a spine stand out.

Tello Obelisk

It is one of the mysterious stone sculptures found in Chavin. It is a 2.52 m high prism, in whose faces there are two great dragons or caimans, one male and one female that according to some scholars, would symbolize the balance of the universe, although there are many other interpretations.

Rich and Skillful

The inhabitants of Chavin were great metal smiths that practiced hammering and embossing, and even worked with alloys of several metals. They obtained gold from different washing places on the affluent of Maranon River.

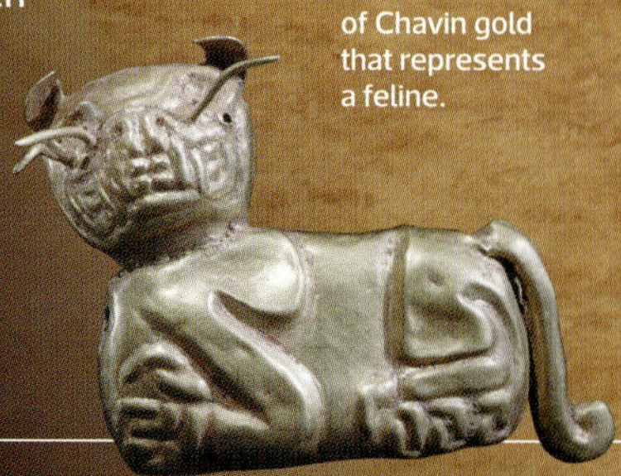

Pendant. Piece of Chavin gold that represents a feline.

VENTS
Light gets in the temple only through a few vents that are believed to be used to listen to the oracle's voice.

Supernatural Acoustics

At around 7 m deep under the Lanzon, in the Old Temple, a network of canals and galleries was found. It is a sophisticated drainage system designed in such a way that when rain fell, a sound similar to the roar of a jaguar could be heard.

TENON HEADS
The temple was full of this kind of sculptures with a terrrorific aspect. They were thought to frighten away the bad spirits. They owe their name to the fact that many of them were nailed to the walls.

Cosmic Axis of the Temple

The Old Temple, built with the shape of a letter "U" and later extended in its south wing, was divided in two by an imaginary axis that joined the two great divine representations: Tello Obelisk, in the center of the round plaza, and the Lanzon, in the inner galleries.

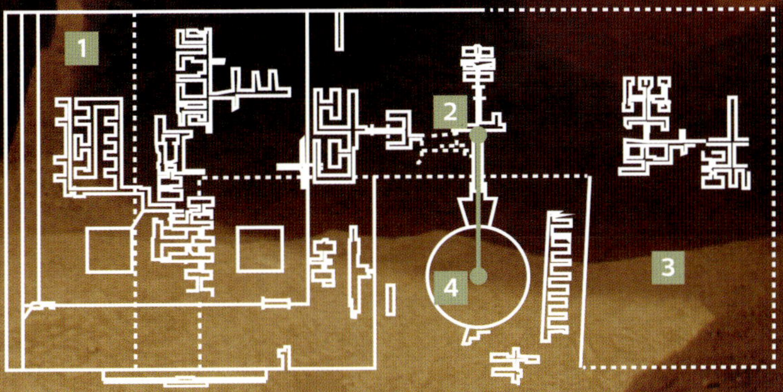

1. New Temple
2. Gallery of the Lanzon
3. Old Temple
4. Round plaza (Tello Obelisk was in the center)

The Origin of Machu Picchu

Much has been speculated about who ordered and for what reason the construction of the mythical Inca city. There are documents that relate it with Inca Pachacutec. It was probably his resting place during his reign and, later on, a sanctuary where his mummy was venerated.

Everlasting Mystery

Having been hidden for centuries and not having written records that describe it, even today there are new theories that try to explain why Machu Picchu was built, and why it was abandoned. It is known that everything happened in a period of hardly 80 years and that its existence had much to do with religious and astronomical beliefs of the Inca, closely related with the most important aspects of their life: fertility of the crops and the animals, political control, trade, etc.

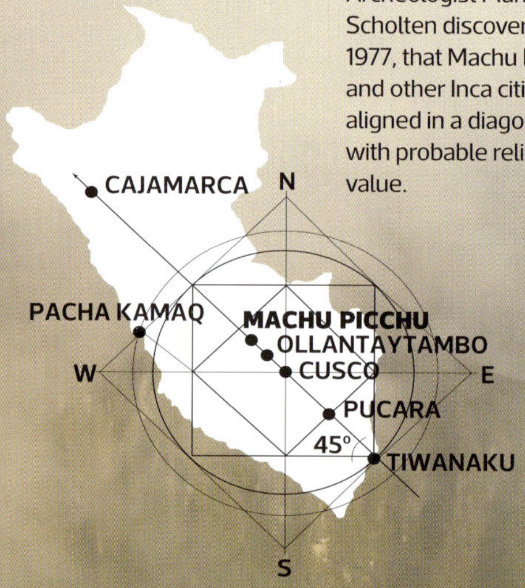

SACRED DIAGONAL
Archeologist Maria Scholten discovered in 1977, that Machu Picchu and other Inca cities are aligned in a diagonal with probable religious value.

Amazing Technique

Machu Picchu is a master work of Inca architecture. Its constructors overcame the difficulty of adapting to an extremely abrupt orography, with very steep slopes. For this, they deforested the area and built platforms or terraces with irrigation canals for crops. The mostly used material was the stone. The most used ones were diorite, porphyry and granite.

WALLS
The carving of the stones and their perfect fit in the walls were a cause of admiration for the Spaniards.

Stone nails. The tree trunks of the roof frames were tied with ropes to nails made of stone.

Who Were the Virgins of the Sun?

A group of women selected for belonging to nobility and because of their beauty, made chastity vows to dedicate themselves to the role of wives of the Sun god. They were the Virgins of the Sun, term created by the Spanish conquerors. They were also called "*acllas*" and were recruited from all around the territory at an age of eight years, receiving a meticulous instruction from a priestess.

Chosen maidens. Statuette of a Virgin of the Sun found in a high sanctuary. Sometimes they were sacrificed as part of the ritual known as "*capacocha*."

The Decline of the City

The conquest of Cusco by the Spaniards in November of 1533 marked the decline of the city of Machu Picchu. It is believed that the few inhabitants that were still there escaped so they would not face the conquerors, although it Is not known exactly.

Abandonment. The temple that guards the Intihuatana, in a picture taken by Hiram Bingham's expedition that rediscovered Machu Picchu In 1911.

THE INTIHUATANA
Some researchers think that the Inca sculpted this sacred stone copying the shape of the Huayna Picchu mountain, located behind the Inca city.

Sanctuary and Observatory

According to Spanish chronicler of the 16th century Juan de Betanzos, Machu Picchu was a sanctuary dedicated to the veneration of the Inca Pachacutec's mummy, who ordered building the city. However, there are buildings that make you think it might have been an astronomical observatory, like the Intihuatana, mysterious sacred stone set on a hill, to which you could have access through a stairway.

The City of the Gods

Teotihuacan, the largest urban center of the pre-Hispanic America reached its peak between 450 and 650 AD, but in the next century, it declined quickly and mysteriously, and many puzzles remain unanswered.

The Origin of Teotihuacan

Researchers agree that Teotihuacan was born as a result of population movements, possibly with an Otomi, Chichimeca, Chocho-Popolocan or Proto-Nahuan origin, which took place during the centuries preceding our era. The main hypothesis is that the first settlers migrated due to the eruption of volcano Xitle and settled in the valley of Mexico since it was rich in springs, raw materials and fertile land for cultivation. Later, Teotihuacan experienced tremendous growth as a religious and commercial center.

LOST IN TIME
When the Aztecs later arrived at Teotihuacan, the original inhabitants were gone. Signs of fire and violence were found, perhaps caused by a civil war or invasion, but an earthquake or an epidemic are not ruled out as options.

Were There Human Sacrifices?

The rituals during which humans and animals were offered to the gods were common at the start or completion of the construction of temples. Remains of 1,228 burials have been found and many of them correspond to sacrifices (see Teotihuacan gods on the right). In general, the victims were beheaded.

Quetzalcoatl
Known as the Feathered Serpent, this deity is related to agricultural cults and human sacrifices.

Huehueteotl
It was also known as Old God and God of Fire. He was portrayed as an aged man with a brazier shape.

Tlaloc
God of water, responsible for forming clouds and lightning. Its gender is both male and female.

Chalchiuhtlicue
She is the goddess of water from rivers, lagoons and sea. She was also associated with fertility.

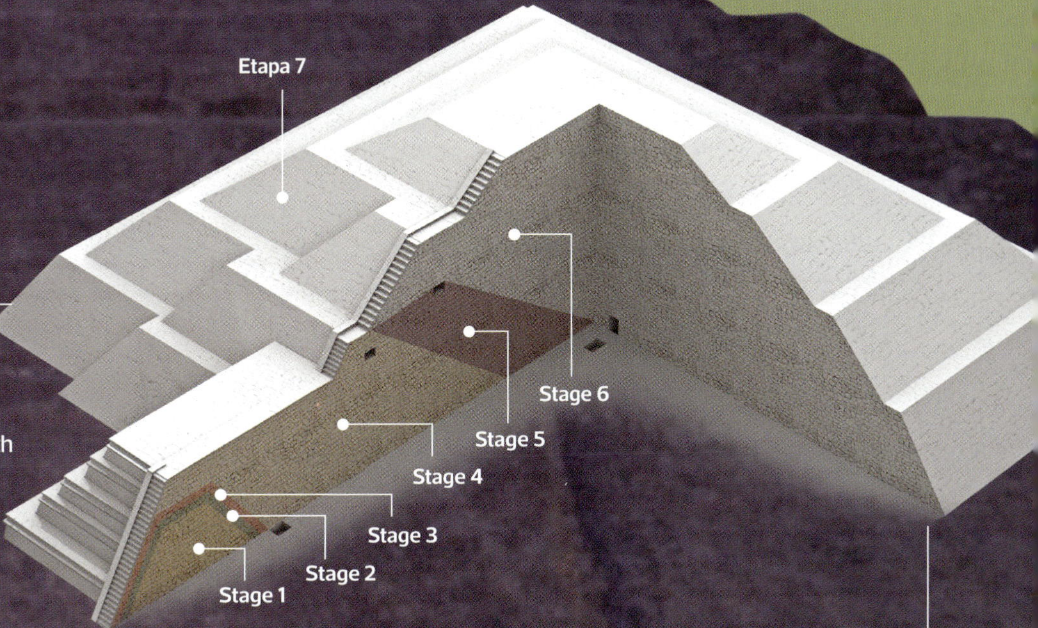

Teotihuacan Pyramids

Some say they share a special symmetry with the pyramids of Egypt, as regards position and orientation. One of the main ones, the Pyramid of the Moon, is a massive building which was built in different stages over several decades.

1 Location
They first selected and flattened the ground and then delimited the foundation with walls.

2 "Drawers"
They assembled "drawers" of mud bricks and filled the gaps with stones and mud.

3 Covering
They covered the filling with a layer of small stones and a layer of concrete.

4 Edges
They were finished as slopes with flat slabs of stone and the process was repeated on the following levels.

5 Retouching
Some parts were polished and coated with a layer of stucco, which could be colored.

Network of Tunnels

A complex system of wells and caves linked the Teotihuacan people with the underworld and the stars. The underground area was sacred and it was used for the offerings of priests. Some of these galleries are the result of natural geological processes, but many other were excavated and modified.

Underground. In 2010, a passage was discovered 12 m below the Temple of the Feathered Serpent.

The Nazca Lines

At about 450 km south of Lima (Peru), the famous Nazca geoglyphs were discovered almost a century ago. Since then, researchers have wondered, with no clear answers, how these mysterious lines were made and what purpose they had.

Perceivable Only from the Air

It is amazing that these lines and symbols can only be seen in their entirety from the air, flying over the desert, which has raised big questions about the intentions and abilities of their authors. It is believed that these huge lines and figures were the way chosen by the Nazca civilization to send messages (offerings and petitions) to the gods in heaven.

For best viewing, lines and geoglyphs are not drawn to scale.

DIVERSITY
The variety of the geoglyphs is one of the main features. Animal and plant figures coexist with rectangular and triangular avenues.

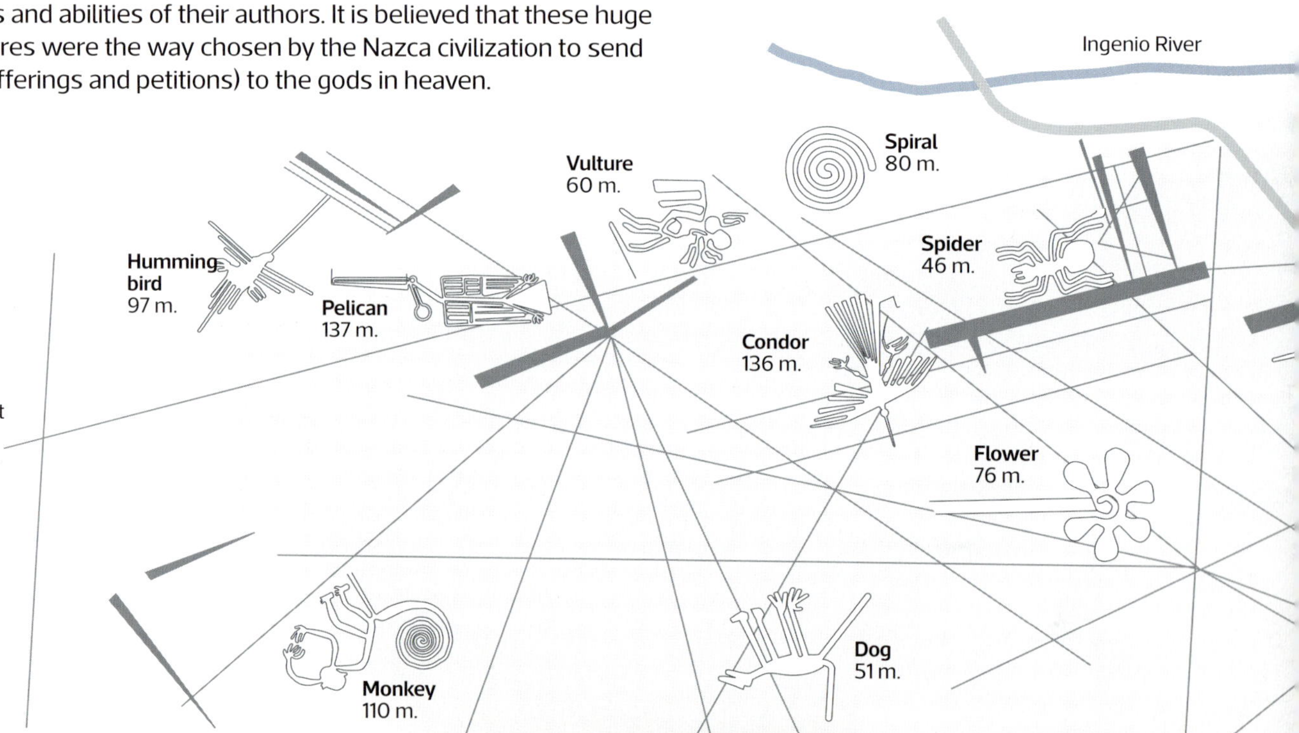

How Were They Drawn?

The most widespread theory is that one supported by researcher Maria Reiche, author of these sketches: the picture would have been made in sections, using a measurement unit to transfer it to the land.

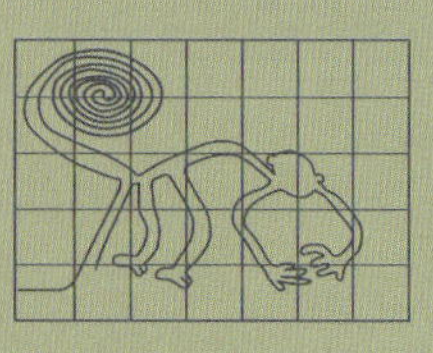

1 Scale
Firstly, the had to prepare a small-scale drawing to serve them as a model, which would be divided into sections.

2 Measurement
Then, they probably used a unit of measurement that may have been applied by expanding a string into radial segments.

3 Projection
Finally, they would have transferred the design to its actual size, tracing the areas and reproducing the lines, section by section.

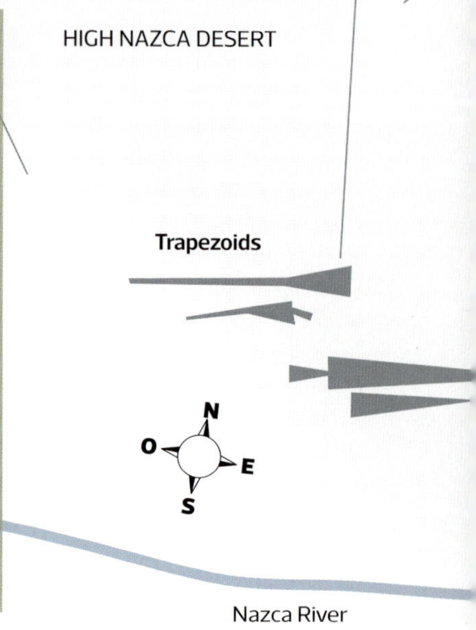

Also in Crafts

There is a clear relationship between the iconography of Nazca craftsmanship and the lines and gigantic geoglyphs in the desert. For example, the hummingbird, a bird with sacred character that augured good crops, was present in large geoglyphs and also in ceramics, typically associated with natural elements such as flowers or grown seeds.

Ceramics. Both the hummingbird and the flower are represented in the lines and in the pottery of Nazca.

How Did They Resist Wind and Rain?

It seems a miracle that the Nazca lines have survived the ravages of time. One possible explanation is that rainfall is very low in the area, and while the pampa of Nazca is windy, the dark color of the soil and the high temperatures form a hot air cushion that slows the wind at a few inches above the soil, protecting the surface from erosion.

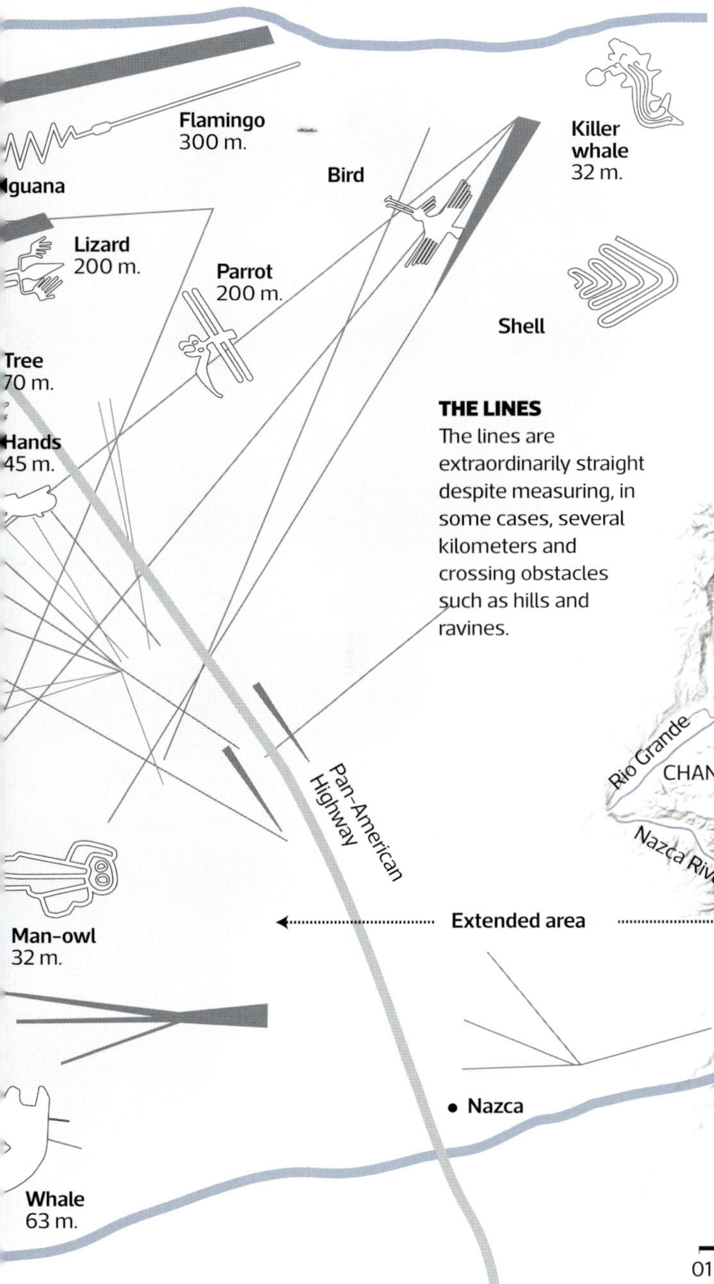

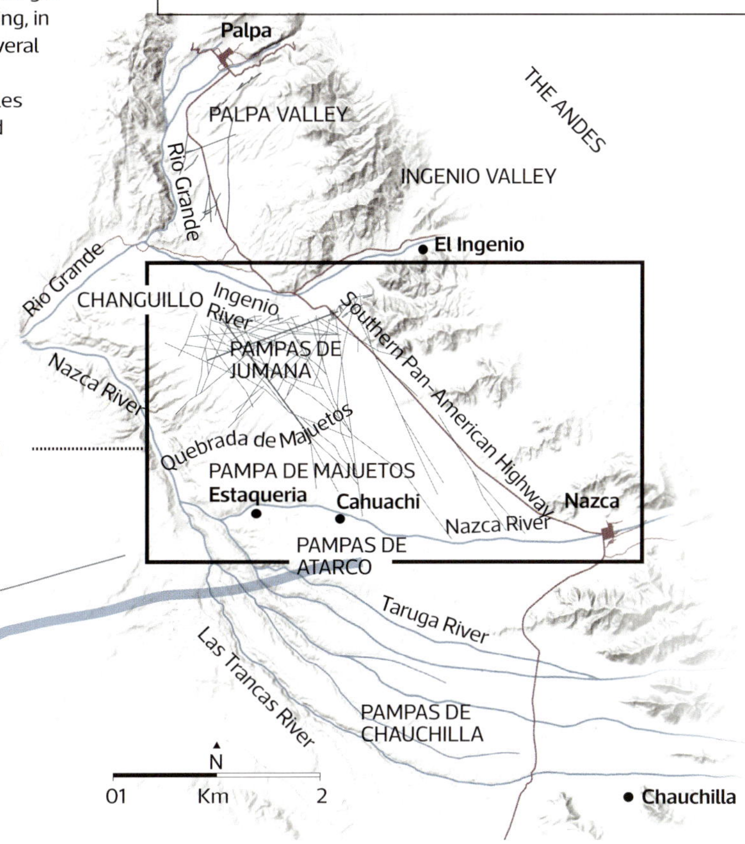

The Secret of the Moai

There are still great uncertainties about the system employed by the natives of Easter Island to erect and mobilize its gigantic sculptures, the moai. It appears they used wooden sledges and very resistant ropes.

Large-scale Sculpture

Thanks to the analysis of the numerous unfinished moai found in the quarry of Rano Raraku volcano and those which were abandoned in various parts of the island during the transportation process, hypotheses have been developed about how these great figures of stone were carved, moved and placed. The volcanic rock was cut with basalt tools and shaped in the quarry. The sculpture was transported either upside down, sliding it over logs, or standing, using ropes and levers.

STONE RAMPS
Once in the *ahu*, the Rapa Nui would gradually lift the moai through the accumulation of stones beneath the sculpture, forming a ramp.

How Did They Get to the Island?

The customs, utensils and crops or the dialect that was observed by navigator James Cook when he reached Easter Island in 1774 suggest that the Rapa Nui came from other islands of Polynesia. Thanks to his navigation knowledge and his double hull vessels, the Polynesians colonized many Pacific islands.

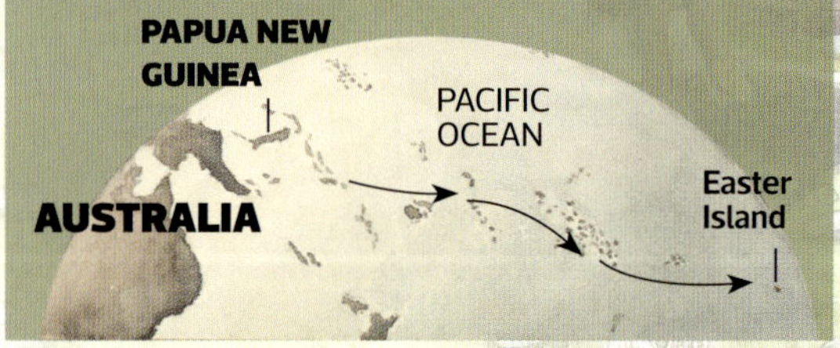

The Step by Step Process

1 Chiselling
The moai was chiselled face-up, on the volcanic rock. The back was not carved, to drag it down the slope.

2 Transfer
The statue was removed and then it was dragged by ropes down the slope to the foot of the volcano.

3 Digging the pit
It was taken to a pit dug to erect the sculpture, with the help of plant ropes and wooden levers.

4 Opening of the pit
After honing the neck and back of the moai, the gap was released to continue with the transfer. The soil was smoothed.

CORONATION
Once the moai was erect, they proceeded to its "consecration": coral eyes were placed and the sculpture was crowned with a *pukao*.

CONTROL
Skilled craftsmen who were part of the caste of nobles controlled the progress of the work.

LEVERS
One or more levers were slid on each side of the moai, between the stone ramp and the sculpture, to progressively tilt it towards the platform.

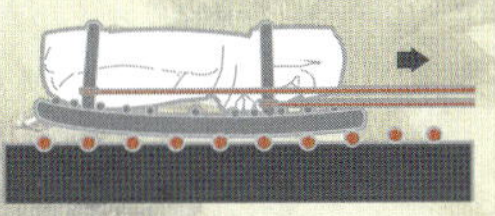

5 Transport
The sculpture was placed and transported upside down, on a wooden sledge that slid over logs.

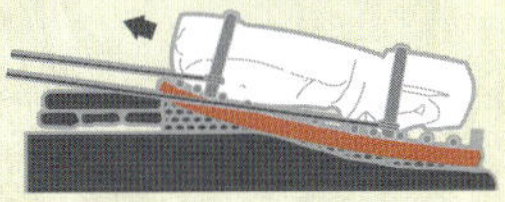

6 Positioning
At the *ahu*, stones were piled under the base of the Moai to lift the sculpture to the pedestal level.

7 Lifting
Using levers, more stones were piled up to form a mound that would erect the moai.

8 Standing
Another theory is that the moai were moved and placed standing by swaying it, with the help of ropes.

The Decline of the Mayas

Years ago, the decline of the Maya civilization was attributed to natural disasters or deadly epidemics. Currently, researchers are inclined to believe in a combination of factors: drought, overpopulation, resource depletion and war.

Environmental Collapse

The demise of one of the great pre-Columbian cultures is a topic that continues to intrigue scholars. The prevailing opinion is that the end of the Maya cities was due to an environmental crisis caused by human activity. Massive deforestation would have produced a drought, exacerbated by the general global warming. This would have led to shortages of food, water and firewood, while the various kings confronted each other for the best land, which caused chaos at all levels.

Great Plaza of Tikal. The temples of this great Maya city still rise majestically above a sea of jungle vegetation.

TEMPLE I
Also called the Temple of the Great Jaguar due to the jaguar carved on the lintel of the main entrance, it was built in 700 by King Jasaw Chan K'awiil I to house his tomb.

Who Burned the Maya codices?

Everything indicates that it was the Franciscan monk Fray Diego de Landa who sent the Maya codices to the bonfire, which he regarded as the devil's work, eliminating valuable information about that culture.

Detail from a Maya codex.
Museum of the Americas, Madrid, Spain.

Maya Chronology

Archaeologists distinguish three major stages in the history of the Mayas: the Preclassic (from 1000 to BC to 300 AD, a period of formation), the Classic (from 300 to 900, where the largest blooming of such culture took place) and the Postclassic (from 900 to 1697, with the latest Spanish conquests).

11000 BC

Ancestors
The first groups of nomads and hunters appeared in the Yucatan and Peten region, and created irregular settlements.

3114 BC

Onset of the world
According to the Maya calendar, on this date (for them, the 0.0.0.0.0) our era commenced.

h. 2000 BC

In Mexico
Emergence of the Maya civilization in the Gulf of Mexico. Around 1500 BC, the Olmec culture appears.

300 BC

Dynastic Lines
The Mayas adopted the idea of a hierarchical society ruled by nobles and kings, which results in the emergence of dynastic lines.

400

Rise of Tikal
The Maya highlands fell under the rule of Teotihuacan. Tikal became the first great Maya city.

426

New Copan
K'inich Yax K'uk' Mo' established a new dynasty in Copan, which turned the city into one of the most powerful states.

The Mayas and the End of the World

The apocalypse supposedly predicted by the Mayas rested on a date from their calendar that corresponds to December 21, 2012. On said date, a long 5,125-year Maya cycle or era was completed, but it is not clear that they had associated it with the end of the world or some other catastrophe, as claimed by several books. Finally, on such date, that was not the outcome.

DOOMSDAY?
The god Kukulcan (or Quetzalcoatl), representation of Venus and the creator of mankind, in its shape of morning star, arising from the jaws of the serpent of the earth.

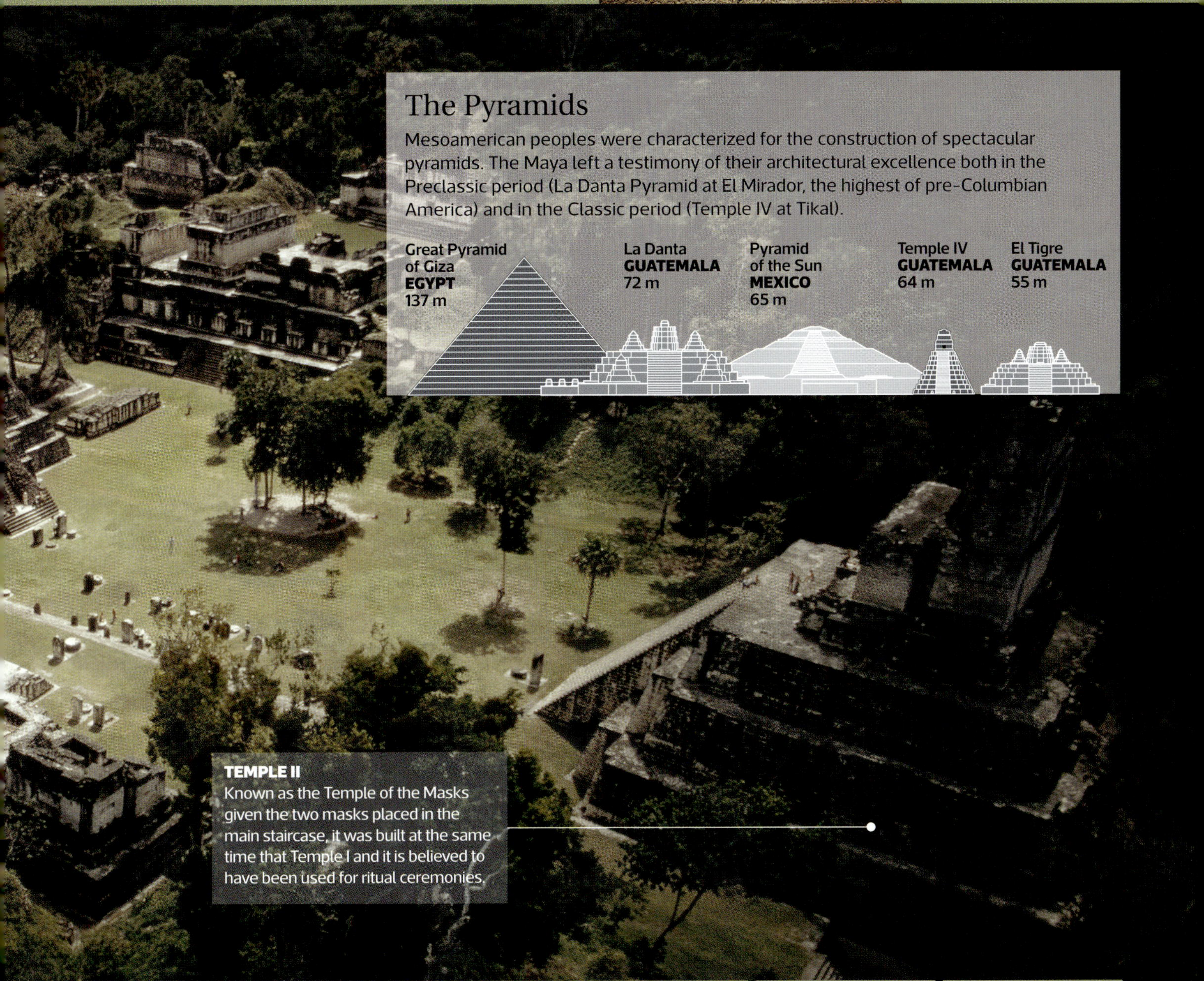

The Pyramids

Mesoamerican peoples were characterized for the construction of spectacular pyramids. The Maya left a testimony of their architectural excellence both in the Preclassic period (La Danta Pyramid at El Mirador, the highest of pre-Columbian America) and in the Classic period (Temple IV at Tikal).

Great Pyramid of Giza
EGYPT
137 m
La Danta
GUATEMALA
72 m
Pyramid of the Sun
MEXICO
65 m
Temple IV
GUATEMALA
64 m
El Tigre
GUATEMALA
55 m

TEMPLE II
Known as the Temple of the Masks given the two masks placed in the main staircase, it was built at the same time that Temple I and it is believed to have been used for ritual ceremonies.

615
Pakal Stage
Pakal, who rebuilt the city, began his reign in Palenque. Pakal governed for almost 70 years, up to 683.

800
End of Tikal
Construction ceased in Tikal and the city was abandoned. The collapse of the southern cities began.

1200
Desertion
Northern Maya cities were abandoned. The Toltec evicted Chichen Itza, which was then occupied by the Itza.

1441
Mayapan
An internal struggle ended with the Maya city of Mayapan, which had hegemony in the Yucatan Peninsula.

1500
Invaders
Arrival of the Spanish people at the Yucatan beaches. They brought diseases unknown and deadly for the Maya.

1697
Last City
The last independent Maya political entity, Tayasal, capital of the Itza, was conquered by the Spanish.

Civilizations of the Amazon

The Amazon River basin, one of the most unexplored regions of the planet, begins to reve its secrets. Very recent archaeological investigations seem to confirm the existence of civilizations that would have brought together thousands of people.

Findings in the Jungle

Conquerors, explorers and adventurers have ventured into the Amazon in search of lost cities, constructed by a civilization that disappeared without a trace in history. To many experts, the archaeological remains found and the analysis of soil strata, showing eras of great fertility and cultivation, are proof that there were one or several complex and developed civilizations that learned to live with the jungle and to dominate it.

Kuhikugu. Recreation of one of the cities that has provided more details about the way of life of the ancestors of the tribes that now inhabit the Mato Grosso.

1 SAN MARTÍN DEL TIPISHCA
One of the villages, out of almost a hundred settlements in the Pacaya Samiria Reserve, where soils enriched by man have been found.

2 EL BENI, BOLIVIA
In this region, archaeological works have discovered roads, high lands for growing crops and canals built in the rivers around 1200 AD.

3 XINGU
Located in the Mato Grosso, this national park contains the remains of a series of interconnected circular cities, proof of the presence of an ancient civilization.

4 ISLAND OF MARAJÓ
In the largest river island in the world, important remains of pottery were found. It is believed that it was a major urban center, inhabited by 100,000 people.

5 GEOGLYPHS
Deforestation in Bolivia and Brazil has exposed geometric geoglyphs with a width of up to 100 m and performed with great precision.

Was the Jungle Soil Enriched?

A new enigma puzzles researchers. In the Amazon basin, extremely fertile land parcels have appeared. It is *terra preta*: a rich blend of nutrients created by man. The big question is: Was it produced intentionally to improve soil fertility or was it an accidental discovery or an involuntary result of human settlements?

Terra Preta. Professor Eduardo Neves (blue shirt) and his team look over a pit dug in the terra preta.

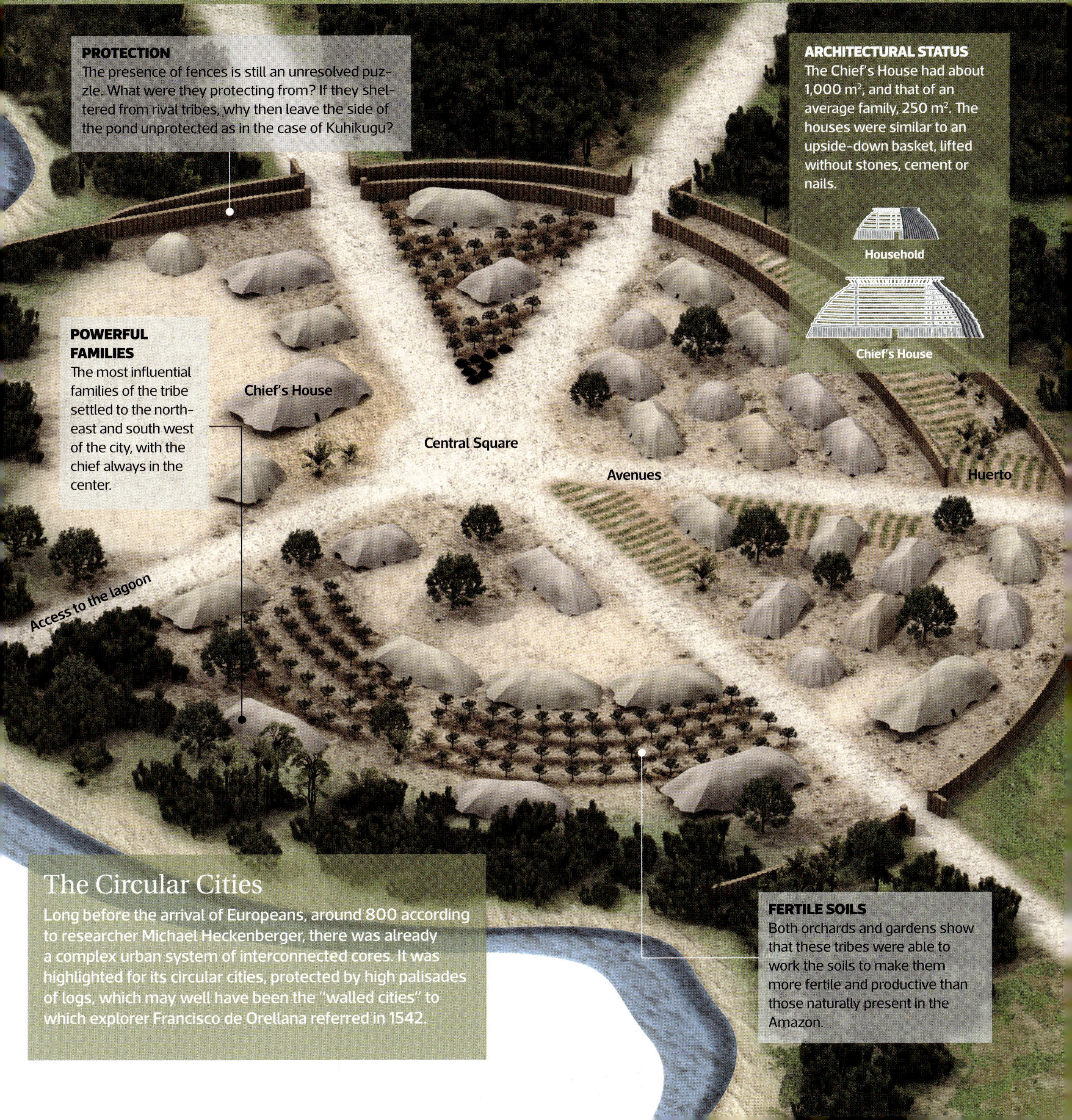

PROTECTION
The presence of fences is still an unresolved puzzle. What were they protecting from? If they sheltered from rival tribes, why then leave the side of the pond unprotected as in the case of Kuhikugu?

ARCHITECTURAL STATUS
The Chief's House had about 1,000 m², and that of an average family, 250 m². The houses were similar to an upside-down basket, lifted without stones, cement or nails.

POWERFUL FAMILIES
The most influential families of the tribe settled to the north-east and south west of the city, with the chief always in the center.

FERTILE SOILS
Both orchards and gardens show that these tribes were able to work the soils to make them more fertile and productive than those naturally present in the Amazon.

The Circular Cities

Long before the arrival of Europeans, around 800 according to researcher Michael Heckenberger, there was already a complex urban system of interconnected cores. It was highlighted for its circular cities, protected by high palisades of logs, which may well have been the "walled cities" to which explorer Francisco de Orellana referred in 1542.

The Legend of El Dorado

Since the 16th century, numerous witnesses have testified to the existence of El Dorado, the mythical American city of gold, somewhere in Colombia, Peru, Ecuador or the Amazon rainforest. But search expeditions have been performed without success.

Going for Gold

The legend goes back to the first Spanish conquerors, to whom the Indians had spoken about the existence of a place where gold was so common that its inhabitants despised it and even the streets were paved with such precious metal. The narrations of the 16th century relate the city of El Dorado with the Guatavita Lake in the eastern range of Colombia, where the Muisca people made great offerings of gold. Spanish and English people explored this and other areas, and even came to drain the lake, but they never found El Dorado.

The Muisca Raft

This famous figure was found in 1969 inside a ceramic pot in a cave in the municipality of Pasca (Colombia). The Raft, made of gold by Muisca craftsmen, refers to the legend of El Dorado since it represents the investiture ceremony of the chiefs of said tribe, which was held in Lake Guatavita.

In the Gold Museum in Bogota. The raft measures 19.5 x 10.1 cm and was carved between 1200 and 1500.

Spanish Expeditions

The Spanish performed at least twenty expeditions to find El Dorado. In 1535, Belalcázar Sebastian searched for it in the south-western area of the northern Andes, near Colombia, like Gonzalo Jimenez de Quesada, who tracked the territory of the Muisca people one year later. However, the most famous of these expeditions was that launched in 1541 by Gonzalo Pizarro and Francisco de Orellana, for it meant the discovery of the Amazon River.

Gonzalo Jiménez de Quesada

Sebastián de Belalcázar

Gonzalo Pizarro

Francisco de Orellana

What Is Manuscript 512?

In 1753, a Brazilian expedition led by Francisco Raposo and Joao Silva Guimaraes, walked into the jungle of the current state of Bahia in search of the Muribeca mines. The rich seam was not found, but they discovered a lost city, the Cyclopean and Greco-Roman architecture of which was described in a writing sent to the viceroy, the so-called Manuscript 512. It is believed that the city could be El Dorado.

The Document. Manuscript 512 was found in 1881 in the catalog of the Brazilian History Exhibit. It is preserved in the National Library of Rio de Janeiro.

Raleigh's Theory

English aristocrat and sailor Walter Raleigh placed the city of El Dorado on the shores of imaginary Lake Parime near the Essequibo river, in Guyana. In 1595, Raleigh made an expedition in the area, but did not find the golden city. On his return, he wrote a book filled with fables that helped spread the myth of El Dorado.

A Golden Chief

According to the narrations of Juan Rodriguez Freyle in his historical and traditionalist chronicle on the colonisation of the Vice-royalty of New Granada in El Dorado, the Muisca people crowned their chiefs in Lake Guatavita, literally covering them with gold dust and making great offerings to their gods.

The Acre Geoglyphs

In Brazil's Acre region, deforestation has exposed some strange symbols carved into the ground, like the Nazca lines. No one knows who created them or what they mean, but they prove the existence of an advanced culture.

The Mark of a Great People

According to the team of scientists that studied the virtually 300 geoglyphs found in the region of Acre, the domain of geometry and the dimensions of these symbols (some reaching 300 m in diameter) demonstrate the existence of a sedentary and organized society, able to work in cooperation. It is not known if the figures drawn on the ground were messages for the gods, delimited ceremonial places or if they had a ritual, defensive, logistical or purely administrative nature, but it has been estimated that that they were the creation of a large society of at least 70,000 people.

LARGE DITCHES
The drawings are made on the basis of trenches going from one to four feet deep and twelve feet wide, dug into the ground.

MUD WALLS
The land that was extracted by digging the trenches was used to make mud walls marking the outline of the figures. Although it was one of the hypotheses, it is believed that these constructions had no defensive function.

Three Figures

Discovered in Rio Branco (Brazil), the geoglyph of Fazenda Colorada is one of the most complex since it joins three geometric figures. This structure suggests that the inhabitants lived on three adjacent squares.

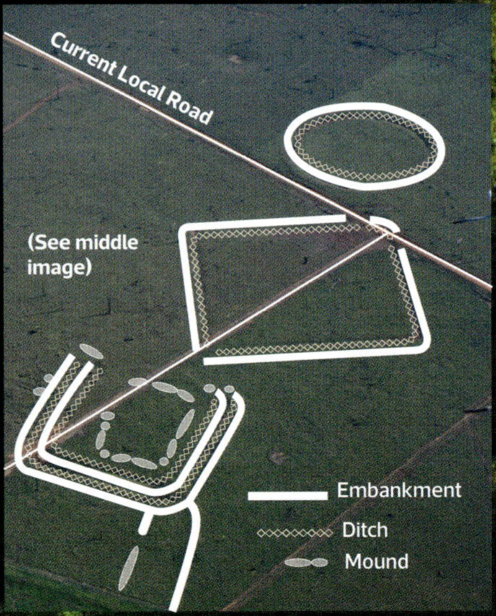

Discovery

Although some of these geoglyphs had already been described in 1977 by Brazilian archaeologist Ondemar Dias, it was Alceu Ranzi, geologist and palaeontologist of the University of Acre who made them known in the mid-80s, after flying over this Brazilian region, near the border with Bolivia and Peru.

CERAMICS
In the trenches of the geoglyphs, ceramic objects were found, such as this glass-mask (Rubber Museum in Acre).

Fazenda Colorada. Central figure of the geoglyph thus named, found in Rio Branco (Brazil).

Dating

Some analyzes performed using the carbon-14 method have dated some organic remains found in the geoglyphs as pertaining to the 13th century, but it is believed that the culture that built them could have inhabited the Amazon a millennium earlier.

DEFORESTATION
The geoglyphs were made at a time when there was no rainforest in the region, whether through human action (as today) or due to environmental causes.

Work of the Incas?

Archaeologists do not rule out that the geoglyphs were the work of Andean communities settling in Acre during the expansion of the Inca Empire. It is possible that Inca leaders sent colonists to settle in the rainforest, from Cuzco or other parts of the empire, such as the Pacific coast, where there are numerous geoglyphs.

Colonizing civilization. Current representation of Inca warrior.

Glossary

ANTHROPOMORPHOUS Something that is human in form or nature.

ASCETIC Someone who practices severe self-discipline.

AUTOPSY An examination to discover the cause of death or the extent of disease.

CODEX An ancient manuscript text in book form.

DRUID a priest in the ancient Celtic religion.

ENIGMATIC Something that is difficult to interpret or understand.

ESOTERIC Something that can only be understood by a small number of people with a specialized knowledge or interest.

FRATERNAL Related to a brotherhood.

FRESCO A painting done in watercolor on wet plaster so that the colors penetrate the plaster and become fixed as it dries.

GEOGLYPH A large motif typically formed by elements of the landscape, such as stones, stone fragments, live trees, gravel, or earth.

HEMOPHILIA A medical condition that reduces the ability of the blood to clot.

HERETICAL Being against generally accepted beliefs.

HIERARCHY A system in which people are ranked according to status.

ICONOGRAPHY the visual symbols in a work of art.

MONOLITHIC A large, powerful, and intractably indivisible system or organization.

NEOLITHIC The later part of the Stone Age.

OBELISK A stone pillar set up as a monument or landmark.

OCCULT Beliefs or practices that are supernatural, mystical, or magical.

PALEONTOLOGIST Someone who studies fossils to determine the structure and evolution of extinct animals and plants.

RADIOGRAPHY An imaging technique that uses electromagnetic radiation to view the internal structure of an object.

SARCOPHAGUS A stone coffin.

TOMOGRAPHY A technique that uses X-rays or ultrasound to display a cross section through a human body.

For More Information

Brown University

Department of Egyptology and Assyriology

Providence, RI 02912

(401) 863-1000

Website: https://www.brown.edu/academics/egyptology

The Department of Egyptology and Assyriology explores the histories, languages, cultures and sciences of ancient Egypt, Mesopotamia and their neighbors.

Central Intelligence Agency

Office of Public Affairs

Washington, D.C. 20505

(703) 482-0623

Website: http://www.cia.gov

Created in 1947, the Central Intelligence Agency is tasked with gathering, processing and analyzing national security information from around the world.

The Grand Egyptian Museum

Administration & Conservation Center

El mathf El masry El Kebir st

El Zobat Buildings, El Remaya Sq.

Giza, Egypt

+ 202 33 776 893

Website: http://www.gem.gov.eg

The Grand Egyptian Museum neighbors a timeless wonder, the Giza Pyramids, and pays homage to eternal Ancient Egyptian monuments, treasures, and history hosting over 100,000 artifacts, about 3500 of which belong to the famous King Tutankhamen.

Machu Picchu Museum

320 Santa Catalina Ancha

Cusco, Peru 080101

(051) (084) 255535

Website: http://www.museomachupicchu.com

The Machu Picchu Museum houses 366 museum-quality objects returned by Yale University in 2011 and the totality of fragments resulting from the excavations, which are kept in storage to be studied by local and international researchers.

Websites

Because of the changing nature of internet links, Rosen Publishing has developed an online list of websites related to the subject of this book. This site is updated regularly. Please use this link to access the list:

http://www.rosenlinks.com/VHW/mysteries

For Further Reading

Aronson, Marc, and Michael Pearson. *If Stones Could Speak: Unlocking The Secrets of Stonehenge.* Washington, DC: National Geographic, 2010.

Bacchin, Matteo, And Marco Signore. *T. Rex and the Great Extinction.* New York, NY: Abbeville Kids, 2010.

Doherty, P. C. *The Mysterious Death of Tutankhamun.* New York, NY: Carroll & Graf, 2003.

Finlayson, Clive. *The Humans Who Went Extinct: Why Neanderthals Died Out and We Survived.* New York, NY: Oxford University Press, 2009.

Krauss, Marianne. *The Unknown Tutankhamun.* New York, NY: Bloomsbury, 2016.

Pearson, Michael. *Stonehenge: A New Understanding: Solving the Mysteries of the Greatest Stone Age Monument.* New York, NY: The Experiment, 2014.

Randall, Lisa. *Dark Matter and the Dinosaurs: The Astounding Interconnectedness of the Universe.* New York, NY: HarperCollins, 2015.

Shipman, Pat. *The Invaders: How Humans and their Dogs Drove Neanderthals to Extinction.* Cambridge, MA: Harvard University Press, 2015.

Wilcox, Robert K. *The Truth About the Shroud of Turin: Solving the Mystery.* Washington, DC: Regnery, 2010.

Wilson, Ian. *The Shroud*. London, England: Bantam, 2011.

Index